MEMOIRS

of a

SPANNER

My Story

notionpress
.com

MEMOIRS of a SPANNER

My Story

Air Cmde K Sanjeevan (Retd.)
(Jeeves)

notionpress.com

Notion Press

Old No. 38, New No. 6

McNichols Road, Chetpet

Chennai - 600 031

First Published by Notion Press 2016

ISBN 978-93-5206-661-2

Contents

Chapter 1

Origins

I was born one morning in a house on a hill near the Arabian Sea in a small town in North Kerala named Tellicherry – a town renowned for its bakeries and beaches, for circus artists and cricket players

It was the season of monsoon, and it appears that it poured continuously for a week after my birth. The date was 17 August 1931.

After my birth, they could not find my birthmark, the position of which on one's anatomy would indicate one's character and future prospects in life. Finally, after searching every inch of my body, they found it as a dark dot in my right eye. Apparently, this meant that the person who has such birthmark would like to have everything he takes a fancy to. The superstition about this across Western cultures was that it was the sign of a witch! However, the effect was compensated by my birth star of 'Atham' which portended good things for the individual, but was not so good for one's parents and siblings. The double whorl on the crown of my head (known as 'eratta chuyippu') was a good sign according to the family astrologer!

My father, KK Achuthan, was a minor government official, like most fathers in Malabar in those days. He was originally from Mahe, a French territory in the heart of the Malabar district (Malabar was part of Madras Presidency and was under British rule). My father's salary was the princely sum of Rs 110 per month, with which he could maintain a Model T Ford, a driver named Moidoo, and two servants, and also pay the rent of Rs 15 a month for a six-bedroom old style house.

My father's grandniece Damayanthi was staying with us. Although her name was Damayanthi, she was known by her pet name, Denthy. She was attending the local college, Brennen College, located close to our house, which was a second-grade college offering the FA course (first year Arts). She later went to Benares University from where she got a BA degree and later an LT (Licentiate in teaching). Naturally, with her LT, she became a teacher. She taught for many years at Mithapur School in Gujarat where her brother Haridas was employed. She remained a spinster throughout her short life, till she passed away of cancer at the Tata Memorial Hospital in Bombay in 1968.

Sending the children outside one's hometown was very rare in those days. There were no colleges providing degrees in North Malabar. The so-called colleges were second-grade colleges offering FA course and later the two-year Intermediate courses after the Secondary School Leaving Certificate (SSLC). There were two such colleges in Calicut: Malabar Christian College and Zamorins College. There was also one in Tellicherry: Brennen College (founded by a British philanthropist Edward Brennen). Few colleges in Malabar, where one could graduate, were Govt. Victoria College in Palghat, or St Aloysius College and St Agnes College for women in Mangalore. As a result of the denial of opportunities for higher education due to the absence of local educational institutions, many bright boys and girls had to terminate their studies after Intermediate (equivalent to Plus 2 now) and join the Post Office as clerks for Rs 105 per month or go away to East Africa, Burma or Singapore in search of greener pastures.

Denthy was instrumental in pet-naming me 'Babu'. My actual name was not a typical Mallu name, but my father had a boss named Sanjeeva Rao whom he used to admire professionally, and he named me after him. I also had a third name called Kunger, which was the name of my grandfather, Kunger Vaidyer, who was an Ayurvedic physician and an expert in curing people with snakebites and who had patients even in the Lakshadweep Islands. Kunger Vaidier's wife, my grandmother, was from the Kunnathidathil family.

My father's designation was 'Overseer' and he was employed in the Public Works Department of the Government of Madras, which, as the name suggests, involved overseeing the construction of roads, bridges and civil works in the district. He was known as Achuthan Overseer, while his boss was known as Koran Engineer. People were known by their job descriptions, this being added after their names to get Achuthan Gumasthan, Bapu Apothecary, Krishnan Dresser, Nanu Compounder, Ramu Writer, Shekaran Master, Choyi Butler, Anandan sub-Collector, etc. In rare cases, the person was just known by his job, like Commissar in Mahe.

I have no memory of our life in Tellicherry. Soon, my dad got transferred to Cannanore, a coastal town about twelve miles North of Tellicherry. I vaguely recall that we were staying in a sprawling house, funnily called 'The Shop'. It was not a rented house but belonged to my father's cousin who was known as 'Kayaniedathy'. I think she was either unmarried or a widow but was very fond of my father. When she died, she left the house and surrounding properties along with a mountain of debt to my father. Adjacent to the shop, there was a shed which was rented out to a bus company called CPC Motors, where the two buses owned by the company were parked during the night. Close to the main road on the Southern side of our house, a pharmacy named BAL & Co was also located on our property. The rent from the Bus Company and BAL & Co added to my father's salary, which put us in what could be called the upper middle-class social bracket.

The house had an enclosed foyer with a room on top. This room was operated as a dental surgery by a dentist named Dentist Vasuettan. He had a brother named Ramdas who used to play with kids like us. Ramdas was unemployed and used to help his brother in the surgery.

On the Northern side of the Shop, on the other side of the road, there was an interesting establishment named FN Heerjee and Sons, which was a petrol pump cum soda shop. The soda was manufactured on the premises and bottled by a vacuum process by which the liquid was trapped inside and sealed with a marble. To open the bottle and have a swig of the soda, one had to put one's left thumb on the marble and smash the marble down with the right hand.

I had two older brothers: Ramdas who was seven years older than me and Bharathan who was five years older. Both of them were students of Municipal High School, located near the Police Maidan. The folks who passed out of this school were considered street smart and were tagged as high school graduates of 'Maidanam University'. The headmaster of the school was the well-known martinet called 'Vala Pattar'. Nobody seemed to know his real name. Many years later, when I used to talk about the old days in Cannanore, I was often asked whether I had been a student of Vala Pattar. I had to confess reluctantly that I never had the dubious distinction of being an alumnus of the august institution presided over by this gentleman. My father had decided, in his wisdom, to put me in the boys section of a Catholic institution named St Theresa's Convent. Boys were permitted only in the 'Lower Infant' and 'Upper Infant' classes, corresponding to the present-day lower KG and upper KG classes. I used to go to school in a horse drawn carriage called the 'Governor's Cart'. Till now, I have not been able to figure out why it was called so, despite googling it and trying various other Internet search engines. These were two-wheeled vehicles drawn by a horse and balanced by the distribution of weight of the load (driver, passengers and goods) over the axle, and then held level by the animal – this meant that the shafts had to be fixed rigidly to the vehicle's body. The horse's lunch, which consisted of freshly mowed grass, was carried in a kind of net attached to the bottom of the carriage. The passengers, usually four, were seated in a white upholstered square coach with a hinged door at the back. You boarded by climbing on the two steps provided at the back. When the Governor's carts were phased out, we had to make do with the humbler Jutka, usually yellow in colour with a curved top, similar to the Tonga of the North The coaches were made by a Madras-based company named 'Simpsons' and after the Jutkas were also phased out, they were used for weddings and film shootings.

The two other kids who shared the Governor's cart with me were a frail, intelligent boy, a distant cousin named Vijayakrishnan and a girl named Jayanthy, who were both in the Lower Infant class along with me. Vijayakrishnan passed away some years later due to consumption and Jayanthy got married to the brother of Denthy, who used to stay with us in Tellicherry. We were given packed lunches from home: mine was what came to be known as 'Choyi's pudding' – crushed ripe plantains mixed with odorous pure ghee and sugar and generously sprinkled with crushed poppadums. I used to insist this as gastronomic delight. This was my packed lunch every day, without fail.

But my days in St Theresa's Convent did not last long since boys were not permitted in the first standard. My father decided to put me in a rather lowbrow school called Kanathur Elementary School, located not far from our house. My teacher was Kannan master, notorious for wielding his cane for the slightest transgression. I survived for a couple of years at this institution, without learning anything other than 'Manipravalam' in Malayalam.

My eldest sibling, Sunanda, was a student of Cannanore Girls High School not far from our house and close to Kanathur Elementary School. She was taught to play the violin at home, besides water colour painting by an Anglo-Indian named Robert Master. He was a kind of Santa Claus in shorts – his sartorial elegance restricted to wearing a pair of khaki shorts, a white shirt and a tie, which accentuated his superannuated appearance. Some of Sunanda's paintings are with her son Sunil in Cupertino, California.

I had two younger siblings: Sarala who was three years younger and Sathyapalan, six years younger to me. Sarala joined St Theresa's Convent after I had left the school and Sathyan was still a baby.

We had lots of fun in Cannanore. One of the persons who tutored me at home was Padmini, my father's sister's grand-daughter. She was being educated by my father. In the matrilineal system in vogue those days known as 'Marumakkathayam', the uncles were responsible to look after their nieces. As a result, one's children were given the same priority as the sisters' children. So Padmini was my father's responsibility.

Marumakkathayam was a system of matrilineal inheritance prevalent in Kerala State. Under the Marumakkathayam system of inheritance, descent and succession to property was traced through females. The mother formed the stock of descent, and kinship as well as the rights to the property were traced through females and not through the males.

Padmini tried her best to teach me the English alphabet although she was not great shakes as a teacher since she herself was linguistically challenged. She had failed twice in the fourth form and had to discontinue her studies thereafter. I did not progress much in the English alphabet department but learnt the Malayalam alphabet quite well. This knowledge got me in trouble with my father in September 1939 when Hitler invaded Poland. Our house had been whitewashed just a month earlier and I could not resist showing off my being up to date with the news. The pristine wall of our verandah was tempting; so, on the whitewashed wall, I wrote in big letters in Malayalam – 'War has broken out in Europe'. When my father saw this, all hell broke loose while he tried to find the culprit. He soon found out who the author of this earth-shattering news was. He tied me to a curry leaf tree and beat the hell out of me.

We lived in a reasonably benevolent environment with occasional hiccups. There was a dead-end street near our house, called 'Mopla Street', where only Moplas (Malabar Muslims) used to live. I used to play with the boys who lived there when they were out on the neighbouring road. They were street smart kids – undernourished, but overcharged with animal spirits. They had a colourful vocabulary, which had the unfortunate side effect of my being prohibited from hanging out with them, as it was thought that it might contaminate my limited knowledge of my mother tongue.

My mother, Janaky, was a frail, delicate, fair lady just short of five feet in height, who was addressed as 'Ammai' (aunt) by my three elder siblings as they had heard her being so addressed during their impressionable years by a number of nieces and nephews who were staying with us successively, some of the time, and simultaneously most of the time. We juniors, my sister Sarala, my brother Sathyan and I, called her 'amma' like normal children, as by the time we grew up, the marriageable nieces got married off and the nephews went off to East Africa and other places in search of jobs and so their influence was not thrust upon us. My mother was from a suburb of Cannanore called Chovva. As the railway station of Chovva was called Cannanore South and since Chovva, despite being only five miles away, was a downmarket kind of place, some of the Chovva walas, including me, had sought deniability of our maternal origins by claiming that we were from Cannanore South. Later on, this subterfuge did not cut any ice with people in general and matrimonial alliance seekers in particular, because Cannanore South lacked identity as a place other than as a humble railway station where mail trains did not even stop, but whizzed past with a long melancholy whistle, and where only goods trains and passenger trains stopped briefly.

My mother had one sister, Narayani, and two brothers, Kumaran and Anandan. Kumaran was the adventurous type and he ran away from home and landed up in the Federation of Malay States (FMS) and managed to get a job in a rubber estate.

There was no news about him for many years until he finally landed up back in India as a confirmed bachelor in 1943 or so. More of him later, as he had a tremendous impact on me as a teenager. My other uncle, Anandan, went away to Burma, got a job in Rangoon, married a girl from Cannanore, sired four children and came back and settled down in Chovva. The house in Chovva was named after him as 'Ananda Sadanam'. The house still exists although a large area of the land around the house had been parcelled out into plots of 10, 15 and 20 cents each and sold off to various Dubai-returned characters.

When my father could no longer continue with his inherited debts, he decided to sell his property, the Shop. Meanwhile, his transfer order came through to Calicut. This accelerated the attempts to sell the Shop and the associated properties. Finally, a Gujarati business man, who lived not far from our house evinced interest and within a week the sale was finalized. Since he did not have ready cash for the entire amount, it as mutually decided that each of the children who were minors would receive Rs 5,000 each on attaining majority. The debts were paid off and we decided to move to Calicut. I collected the 5,000 bucks when I turned eighteen years and gave it to my mother.

We temporarily took a house on rent in a place called Tavakara near the Cannanore railway station till my father organized our stay in Calicut and we finished our school session in Cannanore. Our neighbour was Achuthan Station Master, who was a bigwig in the town. His son Valsettan and my brother Bharathettan became buddies and used to pluck mangoes from the railway yard till they got caught by the Assistant Station Master who threatened to report them to his boss, Valsettan's dad.

As soon as my father had settled down, we moved to Calicut and to a new environment.

Cannanore Beach, 1948

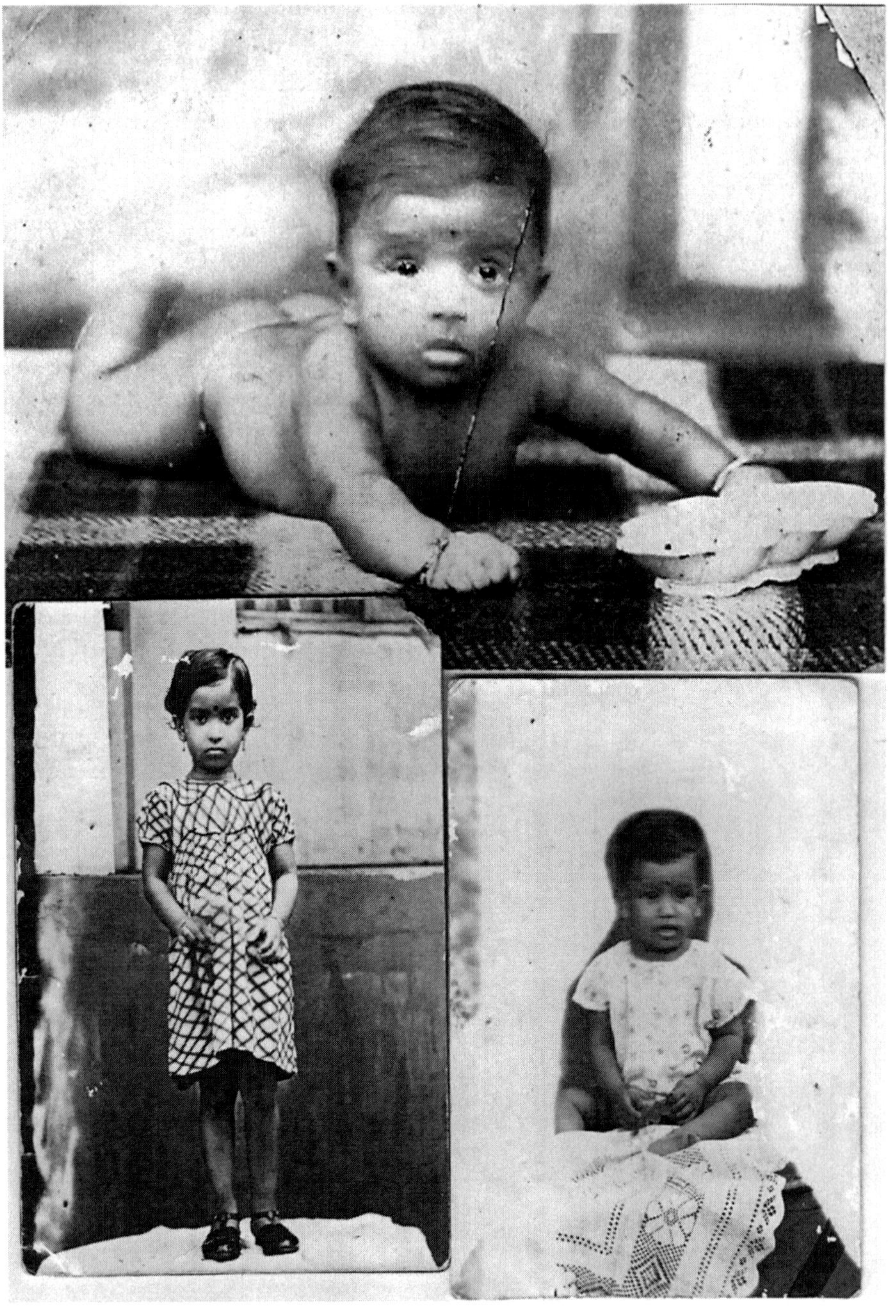

Self, 1931; Sarala, 1938; Sathyapal, 1938

My Father KK Achuthan, 1937

My Mother, CP Janaky, 1964

My Family and domestic staff 1938

Chapter 2

St Anthony's Elementary School Calicut

Calicut (now renamed Kozhikode) has a long and illustrious history of trade, invasions and liberation struggles. It was dubbed the 'City of Spices' for its role as the major trading point of Eastern spices during the middle ages. The Portuguese explorer Vasco da Gama arrived in Calicut in 1498. Calicut was once the capital of an independent kingdom. The Portuguese, Dutch and the British had their presence there at various times.

My father rented a house in Calicut near the third railway gate. Calicut Town had the South-North railway line, which sort of bisected it. There were six manned railway gates in the town. These gates dominated the town in that many localities were identified in terms of their proximity to one of these gates. The first gate and second gate, not far from the railway station, were located near the commercial areas of the town, whereas the third, fourth and fifth gates were near the residential areas. The sixth gate was considered too far away to be of any consequence.

The house named Malikakandy house was very close to the railway line. It was a two-story house with three bedrooms on the ground floor and three on the first floor. There was no electricity and we used oil lamps with very colourful shades.

I was admitted to the fifth standard in a neighbouring school called St Anthony's Elementary School. It was not a fancy school and I have no idea how I got admitted to the 5th standard as I had left the Kanathur School in Cannanore from the 3rd standard. They called it a double promotion, normally awarded to bright students from the same school. I did not qualify on either of these counts. But small things like this can have far-reaching consequences later in life. The school was close by and a boy servant named Appu used to leave me there and bring me back.

There are very few things I can recall about the school. There was a gangly boy named Francis, who had six fingers on each hand. The sixth finger was attached to the little finger and it used to dangle there and we used to delight in playing with it. Another boy named Richard Taveira, who had his home in what was known as 'The Line', was my companion during our walk to and fro from school. His parents were in the copper vessels business and were known as 'Chembootys'. One could see them hammering away on inverted copper vessels and tinning the vessels.

The landlord of our house was a businessman named Imbichi Mudalali. His house, located in the same compound as ours, was called Karumaadath House. He had three children, all of whom were older than me. It was understood that the eldest, Rajan, who had a slight squint, would take over the business. The next one, Sreedharan, would become a lawyer and the youngest one, Haridas, a doctor.

There was another house in the Karumaadath compound, where two boys around my age lived. The elder one, Sreedharan, later joined the Railway Mail Service and the younger one, Divakaran, got a job in the Commercial Tax Department.

On weekends and holidays, all of us would romp around in an old style swimming pool, called 'Kulam' in the vernacular. Those who were new to swimming like me were taught to swim with the aid of two unshelled dry coconuts joined together with a rope and put around the waist to add buoyancy to the body. Some had slightly advanced devices in the form of discarded rubber car tire tubes suitably inflated to add buoyancy. One of the swimming gurus for advanced swimmers was Kumarettan, a relative of the Karumadath folks. He had a business selling firecrackers. His swimming prowess would captivate us, particularly one feat in a running dive with a somersault in mid-air. None of us could graduate to that level but all of us, including my cousins from Ganesh Nivas, learnt swimming in this pool.

The railway line, running North to South, was right in front of our house. The most important train was the Madras–Mangalore Mail going North and the Mangalore–Madras Mail going South. It so happened that folks found the railway line a quick and convenient exit route to end their unhappy lives, usually lovelorn females or examination failures. After the exam results came out, it was a certainty that there would be one suicide either near the third railway gate in front of our house or near the fourth railway gate located a couple of 100 yards to the North.

We had a cousin, Kunnathidathil Vachali Sreenivasan (Sreenettan) staying in our house more or less permanently. He had a job as a stenographer in the office of the Assistant Chief Coffee Marketing Officer, located on Silk Street. His father Anandan Master was my father's elder brother and worked in his hometown Mahe as a teacher in La Bourdonnais College (Mahe is named after the French Naval Captain Bertrand Francois Mahe, Comte de La Bourbonnais who had captured Mahe in 1724). Sreenettan was a secret smoker and would use me as a courier to get him an occasional packet of 'Scissors' cigarettes in return for giving me the labels from the matchboxes which otherwise would be discarded. I had a fairly good match label collection, thanks to Sreenettan.

He retired after many years as the Assistant Chief Coffee Marketing Officer from Manathavadi in the Wynad district of Kerala.

Sreenettan had a younger brother named Haridas who was an artist and had learnt oil painting from Robert Master, who was my sister Sunanda's painting teacher in Cannanore. In fact, he used to stay with us while learning painting. He worked as a draughtsman in Bombay for many years and married a Punjabi lady. Their marriage photo was published in the Illustrated Weekly of India in 1947 or so. They had three daughters, all of whom are settled in Australia. One of them, Rita Surinder is in touch with me on Facebook.

A cousin named Ramakrishnan would have lunch with us on weekdays as he had to commute every day from Elathur. I recall that he became a lawyer later on. His grandfather was my father's eldest brother Jailor Krishnan, who also had his home in Mahe. His son, Cakkat Cunnathidathil Balan (The English initial letter K got converted to C in French) had a brandy shop in Mahe on the main road. His sons have multiplied the business many times since then.

Behind St Anthony's School a distant relative named KK Indran had a house which we used to go frequent. Opposite to his house, across the road, another friend named Henry used to live. We all became buddies and used to play a game called 'Soddi', which faintly resembled the game of kabaddi in Maharashtra.

Another friend during those days was Peter Paul Mendonca, whose parents were also in the copper vessel tinning business and were known as Chembooties. He used to live in what was known as the 'Line', near Richard Taveira's place.

I faintly remember a lovely grotto in the courtyard of our school with the statue of Mother Mary in it. It no longer exists now.

In memories of journeys past, some portions remain stubbornly unavailable for recollection. My days at school at St Anthony School fall into this category probably because it had no great reputation as a school, either academically or in sports, which would stick in one's memory ages later.

Luckily for me, after about a year, my father decided to move me to Malabar Christian College High School that had a much better pedigree.

My father's job as an Overseer involved a lot of travel around the area surrounding Calicut. One of the places he used to visit was Beypore, a suburb of the town, and I used to accompany him and we used to visit his elder sister Nani amma who lived in a massive house called Komath House. The house had an entrance building called Padippura, close to which there was a pond with lots of edible fish. In fact, I learnt line fishing in that pond. Nani amma was married into an agriculturist family and her husband was an adhikari. One of their sons, Damuettan, inherited the title and was called Damu adhikari. On some of our visits, my father would take the family for boat rides in the Chaliyar River. The boat makers of Beypore were artisans of international fame. The boats were known as Uru and the art of Uru making is as old as the beginnings of India's maritime trade with Mesopotamia. Considered arguably the biggest handicraft in the world, the Uru connected this sleepy village of Beypore to the world during the heyday of the spice trade.

The hull and the frame of the Uru are made in a building yard, while fitment of the engine and customization were done elsewhere. On completion, the Uru is launched on the river by *Mopla-Khalasis* (after the Arabic word for dockyard workers), who employ the age-old pulley-wheel mechanism to roll the boat on a bed of logs to float it out.

It was great piece of education for me to see these phenomenal artisans at work.

Occasionally, I would accompany my father to Elathur, a panchayat village, located about twenty-five miles to the North of Calicut. He was involved in the construction of the bridge across the river known as Korappuzha. My father's niece was married to an agriculturist in Elathur who used to live in a house near the bridge called Kallumbarath house, which I vaguely recall had the entire courtyard cemented and on which paddy used to be spread out to dry.

The Korapuzha is generally considered the *cordon sanitaire* between North and South Malabar and the women of North Malabar crossing the Korapuzha and going South and marrying a person from South Malabar was considered taboo.

My younger siblings, Sarala and Sathyan and I used to study and play together. My father devised a simple system of controlling our animal spirits from going haywire. At the end of each day, he would award marks to each of us ranging from 0 to 4. The best behaved would get 4 and the worst would be awarded a zero. At the end of each month, the scores would be added up and a gift would be awarded to the highest scorer. My sister Sarala was the one who got the maximum gifts. I do not recall getting any.

The decision to shift me from St Anthony's School to the Malabar Christian College High School would perhaps have been because of my low scores in this marking system.

Chapter 3

Malabar Christian College High School Calicut

Malabar Christian College was founded in 1909 by the Basel Mission Foundation of Germany and operated by local church organizations. It was a protestant institution, unlike St Anthony's School, which was Catholic and run by Italian missionaries. The first principal of Malabar Christian College was Rev. W Muller who was succeeded by WE Hoare MA (Oxon). When I joined the school in 1942, the head master of the high school was JF Thaddeus. As it was wartime, the British rulers of the country had interned the Germans who the staff of the school.

The college had two major divisions: the college division and the high school division. The college division consisted of the Intermediate sections, the Junior Intermediate section and the Senior Intermediate section. The High School division had classes from 1 to 5 and Forms from First Form to Sixth Form.

I was in the Second Form and my oldest brother Ramdas was in the Junior Intermediate class. My other brother Bharathan was in the Fifth Form.

The campus was located in the heart of Calicut. The Calicut–Kannur highway was on the Western side and the Calicut-Wynad road on the Eastern side. My class was in a shed close to the Wynad highway. The next class was divided from ours by a kind of bamboo woven screen which, while providing visual separation, did nothing to provide audio isolation. The back benchers could make holes in it and talk to their buddy backbenchers in the next class, which often resulted in caning by our class teacher, Kunhappan Nair, who was not much of a teacher but had a terrifying handlebar moustache and luxurious mutton chop whiskers, and was moonlighting as a kalary payattu instructor. I do not recall the subjects he was teaching us, but he was very eloquent in giving us homilies about diet and exercise. I still follow one of his instructions about the technique of drying oneself after a bath. He told us that the first part of the body to be dried was one's back. When asked why, he told us 'yours is not to question why'. We did not; as we knew he could really wield his cane if we persisted in asking inconvenient questions. He also instructed us not to sleep on our left side as the heart was located there and the weight of the right lung was bad for the heart. His advice to us on English essay writing was to keep away from fancy words because you never can tell what they mean.

I had two close friends studying in the same class and sharing the same bench. I was a 'front of the classroom' kind of boy, not because of any academic accomplishments, but because of my lack of inches. The smaller boys were compelled to sit on the front benches and the bigger and usually dimmer guys had to sit at the back. Based on this criterion, KK Indran and 'Kunhon' Henry became my bench-sharing buddies sitting uncomfortably close to our moustachioed class teacher.

One of the happier periods in the school was the Drill Period, for which we were militarily marched off to a sand-filled shed where we could play to our hearts content. The shed was located close to a small road connecting the Wynad road and the Cannanore road. The boundary wall was not very high so we could see the activities happening outside. Besides a roadside vendor selling groundnuts, there was an itinerant seller of something similar to Araldite and his litany which was delivered at the top of his voice was 'American Joint-broken things can be mended' in Malayalam. Henry knew him and during drill class could get him to buy groundnuts from the roadside vendor outside. He had some kind of credit arrangement with him and he would settle accounts with him on Sundays when he came to his house to sell American Joint to his dad while his dad was hydrating his aging cells with coconut toddy.

We also had a rather grumpy teacher named John Master who tried to teach us the Bible. As the marks for Bible were not considered for promotion to the next class, not much attention was paid during his class. In fact, the boys were very unruly during his periods. He had an absurd sense of his own importance. He was instrumental in my relocation to a more discipline-oriented school. It happened like this. Some of us got together during the drill period and decided to rile John Master by collectively coughing as soon as he entered the class during the last period. As everybody would be coughing simultaneously, he could not punish any single individual. It was decided that after ten coughs we would all stop coughing.

As luck would have it, things did not plan out the way we had planned. As soon as John Master entered the class, we all sat in disciplined discomfort awaiting the cue from our ring leader, 'Kunhon' Henry. Shortly thereafter, as soon as he had stopped pontificating on how 'Man's resemblances to the savage are more numerous than his differences from him' or some such crap like that, the collective coughing started, but my cough-counting was faulty and I was found out as the last man coughing. Mission accomplished!

John Master was furious and called me to his desk and gave me a resounding slap on my left cheek. The pain was bad, but the humiliation was worse. He continued with the class and when the bell rang, we all trooped out.

When I reached home, the information had already reached my father through my brother Bharathan's grapevine. He decided to withdraw me from the school and put me in a school with a more controlled environment. He decided that St Joseph's Boys High School, run by Italian Jesuit missionaries, would fit the bill and mould me into a better individual.

I had no regrets for what we had done. There are moments in life when the wrong things you do are the right things to do.

Chapter 4

St Joseph's Boys High School Calicut

St Joseph's Boys School was started in 1893 and run by the Society of Jesus. In 1902, its status was raised to that of a High School and it moved to new premises on Silk Street, not far from the Arabian Sea.

The school's system focused on the overall development of the student, with special emphasis on extra-curricular activities. It had a good football ground which was also converted into a hockey ground just by changing the goal posts and using new boundary lines. The ground was bang opposite to the Boarding House, which was managed by Father Biscaro, who was always accompanied by an Alsatian dog named Gypsy, the school mascot.

I joined my new school on 15 June 1943 and was admitted to the 3rd Form, which had two divisions, Division A and Division B. The class teacher was PL Joseph, who taught us English. Our foundation in English was laid by PL Joseph, who followed the English grammar book by Wren and Martin. His attire was a strange combination of a white mundu, a coat and a tie. He upheld the reputation of the school as being one of the strictest in the area.

The other teacher who made a lasting impression on our impressionable minds was our Geography teacher, MD Joseph. He was fluent in English and was a fast talker. In fact, he was more of an orator than a teacher, and the book he was using to teach us was 'India, World and Empire'. His classes exposed us to the wide wonders of the world.

The students of the school were a combination of Anglo-Indians, Muslims, Parsis and a sprinkling of Hindus. My bench mates were Harold Barboza (the younger brother of Vivian Barboza who later was the Flag Officer C-in-C of Western Naval Command), John Norohna, Zarir Marshal and Dayanidhi Ramchand. Harold later immigrated to Canada after living in England for a few years. He married a Canadian lady and lives in Mississauga, near Toronto. John Noronha, the son of Mr Noronha, our Maths teacher was an outstanding athlete who used to excel in sprint events. After schooling, he and a friend, Alfred Barboza, an alumnus of Guindy Engineering College, undertook an overland journey from India to England by road on a Royal Enfield motorcycle. He has chronicled his journey in a book, a copy of which is with me. He later emigrated to Canada and lives close to where Harold stays. Zarir Marshal was a bright lad, always nattily dressed in white shirt and shorts, and belonged to one of the four Parsi families of Calicut. His younger brother, Darius Marshal still lives in Calicut. Zarir graduated in aeronautical engineering from the Madras Institute of Technology, joined the Defence Research and Development Organization and retired as the Managing Director of Bharat Dynamics, Hyderabad, where he now resides.

Dayanidhi Ramchand belonged to a well-heeled Mudaliar business family and was the son of a famous father, BS Thambi Mudaliar, who owned some sawmills and tile factories in a suburb of Calicut and lived in a large mansion near our school. He would take some of us to his house and he would sneak us inside without the knowledge of his stepmother, of whom he was mortally afraid, to show us some 8-mm adventure films. He later completed his Intermediate from Zamorin's College, Calicut, his BSc from Presidency College, Madras, and later finally engineering from the Loughborough Institute of Technology in the UK. A few years after his return, he was tragically killed in a car accident. He was fond of fast cars and died in a Triumph Mayflower which he had brought back from England.

My sister Sarala had meanwhile joined St Joseph's European Girls' High School next to our school. I have no clue how the school got the 'European' tag. It was a Catholic school run by nuns and was later renamed St Joseph's Anglo-Indian Girls' School. When Sarala joined the school, only 40% of non-Anglos were given admission. A few of them got in by anglicizing their names: thus, Nalini became Nellie, another distant cousin Sarala became Shirley, Malini became Merlin and Bharathy became Beatrice. The school management winked at these sidestepping manoeuvres of anxious parents desperate to get their wards into a good school, partly to increase their academic results and partly for economic reasons. These girls reverted back to their given names after they left the school, as they were reluctant to be saddled with incongruous hybrid names like Nellie Kumaran, Shirley Govindan, Merlin Shivadasan and Beatrice Iyer. It could have hurt their matrimonial prospects too.

My brother Sathyan had also joined St Joseph's Boys School in the elementary section. The three of us commuted to school on foot accompanied by Appu, a boy specifically employed for this and other odd jobs in the house.

My brother Bharathan was hell-bent on pursuing an automobile engineering career even when he was a young boy in Cannanore. He used to hang around the two buses which were being garaged in the shed near our house and occasionally managed to hitch a ride along with the drivers on some of their trips. While studying in the Junior Intermediate class in Malabar Christian College, he found out that an Institution named the Ramakrishna Mission in Mylapore, Madras, was offering a five-year course in automobile engineering. He had such a focused and burning desire to become an automobile engineer that he gave up the Intermediate course and with determined optimism went ahead and joined the course in Madras. My brother Ramdas was already in Madras, where he was doing civil engineering at the Guindy Engineering College.

A year went by and we were promoted to the Fourth Form, which was in high school. In addition to my old friends, new friendships were formed. One of them was Mohammed, the middle brother of three Mopla boys. The eldest was Osman Koya and the youngest was Khalid. All three got admitted to the same class, despite them being a year apart from each other. Mohammed was a bright lad and became a well-known Malayalam poet later in life. He was known by his penname of Kavi Mohammed in literary circles.

We had new teachers now. The Maths teacher, Keshavan Master, made me fall in love with the generally unpopular subject of Maths. He was a natty dresser and would come to school in a well-pressed cotton suit, a different one every other day. He had lost three fingers of his right hand due to an accident and would always have a handkerchief covering it. His conveyance was a man-pulled Riksha, which was well upholstered in white cotton upholstery and pulled by the same man every day. The other new teacher was Harry Master, the Physics teacher, who also came to school in a suit and boots. He was a legendary teacher of science and was an eccentric character. He was actually a lawyer but was teaching us Physics!

We had a bell schedule in school, which was strictly followed by the bell-ringer cum general factotum named Capputty.

Life in school was fun and games. We had meanwhile shifted our residence to a house near the fourth railway gate, next to Ashok Mandir, where our new landlord Rarichan Mudalaly resided. It was during our stay here that we got the electrical connection to our house. It was an exciting day when the lights were switched on and we had to happily relinquish our oil lamps.

During our stay here, my brother Ramdas fell ill in Madras and as his illness did not regress, my father and mother went to Madras and got him admitted to the General Hospital. My first cousin Dr MK Madhavan was doing his internship there and was of great help to them. When his treatment did not have much effect in improving his condition, he was brought home to Calicut for further treatment.

Dr VI Raman of Asoka Hospital treated him for a while without success. My father then tried Ayurveda treatment by Paulose Vaidyar. When that did not work, various other remedies were tried out, including a bizarre one, which involved drinking fresh rabbit blood. Nothing seemed to resolve his medical problem. My father was under a lot of stress and he caught a lung disease called pleurisy.

On 24 September 1944, while I was in class listening to the Geography teacher, Bapputy, the school peon came to the class with a summons for me from the headmaster, Father Saldana. I found my sister along with Appu waiting for me in the headmaster's room. The headmaster told me to go home immediately. We picked up Sathyan from the elementary section of the school and when we reached home we found several relations gathered in the verandah, many in tears. My father had passed away. He was only fifty-two years. We were left fatherless and I had suddenly lost what is known as the dad dividend – the deprivation of a father's love, advice, companionship and security, which one appreciates the value of only when one does not have it.

This was a traumatic event in our lives. We did not have a house to call our own; there was no life insurance, no family pension and not much money.

A few days after the funeral, it was decided that the family would shift to my mother's house, Ananda Sadanam in Chovva and that I would continue in St Joseph's and would stay in my paternal aunt, Devaky Ammamma's house in Calicut named Ganesh Nivas. My father had four sisters, Devaky, Narayany, Kunhimmatha and Parvathy. We were addressing them with ammamma suffixed to their names. Devaky, the eldest of the siblings was left a widow many years back. She was staying at Ganesh Nivas with her oldest son, PK Damodharan, known as Singer Damuettan, not because he was a professional singer – far from it. He was employed in Ceylon by the Singer Sewing Machine Company and had retired and settled down in Calicut after working for the Singer Sewing Company for many years.

Gouthaman was the oldest son of Singer Damuettan and Nithyan was the next, followed by Siddhan (nicknamed Thappan), Asokan and Mythreyan. Bharathy, Bhargavy and Sujata were the daughters. Bhargavy was a great beauty and got married very early. Gauthaman, Siddhan and Asokan remained confirmed bachelors. Damuettan's brother Padmanabhan's (Pappuettan) children, Santosh, Dhruvan, Vasanthan, Shaji, Preman and Vivek were also staying at Ganesh at different times as Pappuettan, a doctor, was a Major in the army and was posted at various military stations located elsewhere in the country. It was a large contingent of boys and girls, great company for me. All the boys used to sleep on the floor in the large verandah in places designated by seniority of age. Besides the children, there were other adults in the house in addition to Damuettan and his wife Sunandedathy. One of them was Balettan (PK Balakrishnan), Damuettan's youngest brother who was a bachelor and was a member of the Communist Party of India. He later became the editor of the Deshabhmani newspaper of the Party (another brother, Sukumaran was also a doctor who graduated in medicine from Saigon and was living in Pondicherry). In addition, two unmarried sisters of Damuettan, Narayany and Thangamma and an unmarried niece, Padmini, were also permanently residing at Ganesh. Thus, we were ten boys varying in ages from four to seventeen years and girls from ten to twenty years living there.

Besides the family members, the other residents were Kunhiraman, a general factotum and an odd job person from Ponnani; Appu, a servant boy with the physique of a body builder; a female cook, Kalyani and a nubile servant girl, Ammalu.

The ladies of the house managed the logistics, the menu, the bathroom protocol, etc. with superb military efficiency. As it was wartime, there was great scarcity of almost everything and food rationing was in force. It was a wonder how they managed to satisfy the metabolic needs of so many young boys, without fear or favour. Rice and wheat were scarce and they managed to make edible things out of tapioca powder and even green banana skins.

My mentor was Thangammedathy, who looked after me, her dear departed uncle's fatherless son, with great affection and generosity of personal attention.

Our school was far quite far away from Ganesh Nivas and since our lunch break was only for an hour, we had to run home barefoot, grab a quick bite and run back to reach school before Bapputty rang the bell.

Everything was hunky dory for a while until one day Bachelor Balettan, who was approaching forty years, announced that he wanted to marry Ammalu, the nubile servant girl. This created a big sensation in the house and there was universal castigation against Balettan, who stuck to his guns and eventually moved out of the house – or was turfed out – we juniors were not privy to what happened. Soon after, he got married to the girl in the presence of some of his Party colleagues, with no family members being present. He was literally excommunicated from the family.

My mother had more or less settled down in Chovva along with her sister Narayani and family. Aunt Narayani was married to Achuthan Gumasthan and they had eight children – five girls and three boys. The eldest boy, Madhavan, had graduated with Sanskrit as the main subject from Annamalai University and had later on went to Tanganyika (now Tanzania after merging with Zanzibar) where he worked for the British government until he retired and returned home. His sister Susheela had also gone to Tanganyika along with her husband, Anandan.

The other sisters and brothers were still studying in various classes. I would spend my holidays in Chovva and had a completely different kind of life there. My bachelor uncle, Kumaran Ammaman had retired from Singapore in the FMS, where he was a supervisor in a rubber plantation managed and owned by the British. He mesmerized me with stories of his life in FMS, his adventures involving the British, the Chinese and the Malays. He had brought a twelve-bore gun and a lot of exotic books and magazines from there. There were two complete series of books by WGM Reynolds: one was titled 'Mysteries of London' and the other 'Mysteries of the Court of London'. He allowed me to read the first one but would permit me to read the second one only after I was above eighteen years of age. I believe the second series were banned in England as it involved the shenanigans of the British Royalty. The magazines were all back issues of the 'Wide World' monthly and were full of real-life adventure stories. It was in one of these magazines that I saw an ad about body building by what was advertised as 'Dynamic Tension' by Charles Atlas. The programme was supposed to be isotonic in nature, which eschewed the use of weights and other gadgets. Another ad which my gullibility made me fall for was 'Pelmanism', which was being offered as a correspondence course from the Pelman Institute of London and advertised as a system of scientific mental training which strengthened and developed your mind just as physical training strengthened your body. It was developed to expand 'Mental Powers in every direction' and 'remove those tendencies to indolence and inefficiency'. I devoured these magazines and believed every word of the colourful advertisements they contained.

After the holidays, I returned to Calicut to continue my studies. Soon, I got promoted to the Fifth Form. My mother meanwhile decided to move to Calicut along with my brother Ramdas and my younger sister Sarala. My youngest sibling Sathyan continued studying in Chovva High School where he soon became the Scout Leader as well as the School Leader. Sarala got admitted to St Joseph's Girls school, Calicut.

We took up a house on rent behind Bapputy Mudalali's bungalow on Veterinary Hospital Road.

I made some new friends in school. One of them was Gobi Albert whose house was behind Revindra Book Depot on Traveller's Bungalow (TB) Road. His mother was a Persian lady and his father was Mr Mohammad Kutty. Gobi had a good collection of the Sexton Blake book series. We would discuss the adventures of Sexton Blake, the poor man's Sherlock Holmes, his assistant Tinker and his pet bloodhound Pedro. On my way home from school, I would go to his house and after ensuring that his mother was not around, he would let me search his wall almirah where his collection of Sexton Blake books were displayed. He would lend me a book on Wednesdays and I would return them on Fridays. Our school followed a five-day week, with Thursdays and Sundays being holidays.

In 1946, I got promoted to the 6th Form, the last and final class in school. One of my new friends was Joseph Jacob, who had recently joined the school along with his cousin PJ Joseph. Joseph Jacob was an ambitious boy, a good student and had an exemplary influence on my academic results. As his parents owned some estates in Wynad, they had taken up a house close to the TB. We used walk together to and from school. We started discussing our future plans after leaving school. Both of us had concrete plans: he wanted to be a lawyer and I wanted to be an engineer. So the first step was to do well in the SSLC examination in March 1947.

I had been doing fairly well in the exams so far. We had three major exams each year: the quarterly, the half-yearly and the final exams. The school had a system of honouring those who passed in all subjects in each of these exams. Their names in order of merit would appear in the honours list, which was framed and displayed in the class till the next major exam when the new list would be displayed. In our class, Barboza, Marshall, Daya and I were regulars on this list.

Two more boys had joined our school during the previous year: George Abraham and K Jaipal. Both were good sportsmen – George in football and Jaipal in hockey. George did his engineering from Guindy and joined the Army and retired as a Brigadier. Jaipal joined the Dufferin and retired as a merchant Navy Captain.

All of us appeared for the SSLC public examination in March 1947. But all our efforts were wasted as the question papers had leaked out in Madras and were even available in Calicut. This became a scandal and tarnished the image of Madras University. Finally, the examination was cancelled and a re-exam was conducted. Personally, it helped me in the Maths paper, as I scored a centum in the subject after the re-exam. So did a couple of others.

We had, meanwhile, shifted to a smaller house in the same area for less rent and soon thereafter, my uncle Kumaran came to stay with us. He had brought his old violin with him which he claimed was a Stradivarius and used to belt out some old tunes on it at odd times of the day and night.

His repertoire of skills was amazing. He used to treat wounds on me and some neighbouring kids by normal bees-wax thoroughly mixed with crushed natural pearls. The mixture was kneaded and flattened just enough to cover the wound. This was applied to the wound and bandaged tightly. After a few days, the bandage would be removed and both the wound and the bees-wax would have disappeared. It was a miraculous piece of indigenous doctoring which he had learnt from an old Chinese medicine man in Singapore.

The SSLC marks obtained by me were reasonably good and would ensure my admission to either of the colleges offering the Intermediate course – The Malabar Christian College or The Zamorin's College. The former was a cosmopolitan college with sports and studies given equal priority. More studious types dominated the Zamorin's College and the students were mostly Brahmin boys staying in the Thali area and members of the Raja family with connections to the Zamorins.

It was decided that I should join the Zamorin's College, mainly because a cousin, Balraj, was studying there.

I got admission into the college in the first group – the Mathematics, Physics and Chemistry group, which was the group required for a subsequent engineering education.

Chapter 5

Zamorin's College Calicut

The SSLC results gave me 385 out of 500 marks, which made me eligible for admission to the Mathematics, Physics, Chemistry group (the first group). The SSLC Certificate was actually a booklet containing the marks obtained in all the final exams from 4th, 5th and 6th forms. I was enrolled in the school as CK Sanjeevan, which, when the initials are expanded, stood for Cokken Kunnathidathil Sanjeevan – the Cokken being my mother's tharavad (ancestral home) and Kunnathidathil, my father's. However, the SSLC Certificate had abbreviated it to Kunnathidathil Sanjeevan, which had happened due to an Anglo-Indian office clerk in the school. While filling up the forms, I lost my first family name, because the Anglo-Indian office clerk tried to rationalize and shorten the long name of this small dark-complexioned boy and just deleted the word Cokken from my full name. Since then all my siblings had the initials CK while I had the solitary K as my initial.

I got admission to the 1st group of Maths, Physics and Chemistry in the Zamorin's college under the principal, Mr Krishaiyer, who had a magisterial presence and radiated a quiet authority. Those who wanted to go in for a medical career would opt for the second group of Botany, Zoology, Physics and Chemistry. The third group was the Arts group comprised of Ancient History, Modern History and Logic. English and a second language were common for all.

We had two outstanding lecturers who made an imprint on my memory. One was our English teacher, MP Shivadasa Menon, an impressive Shakespearian scholar, who besides being highly proficient in English was a regular contributor to the Malayalam weekly, Mathrubhoomy. His articles on wildlife in this weekly were widely read and appreciated throughout Malabar. The other teacher was Mr Ramanatha Iyer, a no-nonsense teacher of Mathematics.

Two of my classmates from school had also joined Zamorin's College along with me. One was Dayanidhi and the other Mohammed Niamuddin, who later became a doctor in Madras, specialized in Ophthalmology. Daya and I teamed up with Dasaratharam Naidu, the son of a businessman who had a big bicycle dealership in Sweetmeat Street (SM Street). We three became inseparable, called ourselves the Three Musketeers and were very focused in our studies. Naidu was a good baseball player as well and as far as I know, this was the only school in Calicut where baseball was being played. One of our classmates in the second group was a brilliant student, CK Jayarama Panicker. He was later a professor of Microbiology and Principal of Calicut Medical College.

We had a great time at Zamorin's, the first co-educational institute I had attended after kindergarten in Cannanore. There were about twelve girls in our group. They were all seated in the front row and almost all of them would wear jasmine flowers in their hair except one Sharada who was a nurse in the Army and was getting further education after leaving the service. There was no communication between the boys and girls, except in the Chemistry lab where there used to be borrowings of bunsen burners and beakers now and then. Intermural romances were supposed to spring up and prosper in places of learning, but such things did not happened among us, but it did between our Physics lecturer Mr PKS Raja and one of his female students whom he married later.

The first year passed and we became seniors in 1948. One of the juniors who joined the college was NK Krishnankutty, whose father, a judge, had recently got transferred to Calicut. He was a bright student and I used to meet him in the public library where he regularly borrowed books by PG Wodehouse. Soon, I too got hooked on to PGW and read almost all his books available in the library. Krishnankutty later joined Guindy Engineering College and after his graduation joined Hindustan Machine Tools at Bangalore, where he rose to be HMT's Deputy Managing Director.

There were many discussions about which colleges to join after completing the Intermediate course. Since there were no professional colleges in Calicut, it was either the Guindy Engineering College, Madras Medical College or Stanley Medical College, all of them located in the city of Madras. Naidu and I were sure of getting admission to Guindy. It was, in fact, my dream, my ambition, my obsession.

We sat for the Intermediate Public examination in March 1949, but as luck would have it, the question papers had leaked out and the exams were cancelled and rescheduled, as had happened in 1947 during our SSLC exam. So, I retreated to Chovva to study and make plans for my future. My eldest brother Ramdas, despite his failing health, had taken up a small job to get some positive cash flow into the family. My sister Sunanda had got married to Mr Madhavan and had moved to Poona, where he was working in the Military Recruiting Office.

My youngest brother Sathyan was doing well in Chovva High School. He was made the School Leader, and had trained in Kalari Payattu. He was the Scout Leader as well. He also stood First in class. My brother Bharathan was at Madras doing his automobile engineering course.

Things were not planning out well for the family financially, and some relatives suggested that I should join the Post Office as a clerk on a salary of Rs 105, which I was not inclined to do.

I got back to Calicut in a confused state of mind and appeared for the re-exam with a penumbra of uncertainty about my future hovering over me. However, I did much better than last time. During the interim period, till the results came out, the three of us – Daya, Naidu and myself started getting autographs from classmates, for which I had got anautograph book specially made from Revindra Book Depot, with coloured papers for each page. Among the girls, we decided to get the autograph of Annapurna whom we considered the best student among the girls. She was the daughter of a famous lawyer named Manjeri Rama Iyer and was living in a house on Annie Hall Road. We went there one evening and knocked on the door, which was opened by Ramaiyer himself. He invited us in and called for his daughter. She was a slim dusky girl and had transformed from a caterpillar into a butterfly during the two years we had studied together. She took our autograph books inside and came back after 10 minutes and returned them. We thanked her and left; and in the lane adjoining her house opened our autograph books to see what she had written. In mine, she had written, 'Be not like dumb driven cattle, be a hero in the strife'. Later, I found out that these were two lines from Longfellow's poem 'A Psalm of life', the relevant stanza of which read,

'In the world's broad field of battle,

In the bivouac of Life,

Be not like dumb, driven cattle!

Be a hero in the strife!'

This advice buoyed up my spirits, which got a further boost when the results came out. I had managed a First Class with Centum in Maths and pretty high marks in Physics and Chemistry. I was told that admission to Guindy would be a cakewalk with this result. After we celebrated our success, I again went to Chovva, where a long letter from my brother-in-law Madhavettan was waiting for me. It was a typed letter and he advised me, considering our circumstances that the best option for me would be to join the Armed Forces of India. He had enclosed a recruiting pamphlet for the Royal Indian Air Force (RIAF), which I went through from cover to cover. I consulted my uncle, my brother and my mother, who were not averse to the idea of my joining the Air Force, so long as it did not involve any flying, which in any case I would not have qualified for, as I did not have the minimum leg length of thirty-nine inches.

After mulling over this for a few days, I took the decision to enlist in the RIAF. It was the best of a set of bad options available for a seventeen-year old at that time. In hindsight, I have no regrets whatsoever for having taken this crucial decision.

Chapter 6

Royal Indian Air Force Depot Hospital Town West, Bangalore

Once the decision was taken, to take a leap into the dark as it were, I started digging up every available piece of information about the RIAF – the options available, the age limits, the physical requirements and the location of institutions for training. The nearest recruiting centre was in Madras. I set out for Madras on the Mangalore–Madras express on 12 June 1949 and reached there on the 13th morning and found accommodation in a seedy looking lodge on Walajah Road near Madras Central Station. Another boy named Stanislaus from Mangalore had also checked into the same lodge. He too had come to join the Air Force.

The next morning we set out to the Recruiting office at Pudupet Lines. The Recruiting officer was Flt Lt Viswasam and he directed us to get our medical check-ups done. I failed in the preliminary check-up itself, as my weight was only 98 pounds and the minimum requirement was 105 pounds. They told me to go back home and return after putting on some weight. Stanislaus was also rejected for some reason and he also decided to go back and try again later. I decided to go to Poona where my elder sister and her husband Madhavettan were staying and try my luck there.

I reached Poona Station early on 15 June 1949 totally clueless about the city or the local language. I hired a Tonga and gave him the address at Tilak Road, where my sister and family were staying. Their apartment was on the 4th floor of the apartment complex and when I rang the doorbell, my sister Sunanda got a shock at my unannounced arrival.

Later, after my brother-in-law arrived, I explained the situation. They said that within a couple of weeks they would ensure that my weight would be brought up to scratch. My brother-in-law's younger sister Padmini (Bhuaji) was staying with them, as she was working in Poona in the Women's Auxiliary Corps (WAC), and she took it up as a challenge to fatten me up. I was given bananas of various types, full-fat milk to drink and lots of falooda and ice cream. By the time D-Day arrived for my recruitment tests, I had almost made it – just short by two pounds.

On the day of the test and medical check-up, I was packed off with six bananas, which I ate just before the medical assistants summoned me for the initial measurements. This extra nourishment made me scrape through the medics. I did very well in the written tests in Maths and English and so was cleared to go to Bangalore for my initial training.

There were four of us selected from Poona: Warren Tully, an Anglo-Indian from Jubbulpore, Henry Fernandes from Poona, Joseph Thomas from Kottayam and myself.

We set off by train and after a couple of days arrived at Bangalore City railway station, using the joint railway warrant given by the Recruiting Office. We were whisked off along with some other boys in a 3-ton truck to Hospital Town West, now called Jalahalli West. Hospital Town West got its name as it was a military rest and recoupment centre for Allied soldiers mainly from the North African campaign. The complex consisting of long barracks was built using Italian Prisoners-of-War as manual labourers.

The Air Force Unit was called the Air Force Depot where we would be imparted General Service Training (GST) and Educational Training for a period of five months after which we would be allotted specific specialist trades based on a psychological and aptitude test known as the psychological screening test (PST).

After the initial kitting and briefings, our training started. I was in No. 2 Flight of No. 3 Training squadron. We were allotted service numbers (mine was 204848) and were serially divided into four batches of about twenty-five in each flight. Each squadron had four such flights and there were four such squadrons simultaneously under training. Ours was the junior most squadron.

Our squadron commander was Flying Officer Thom, a short, smart live wire. There was a Sergeant in charge of each flight, ours being Sgt Abraham, who was a physical fitness and drill instructor (PF&DI). Under him was the hands-on drill instructor, Cpl Dharman, also a PF&DI. There was surreptitious talk among the trainees that these two were AC/DC types. Henry Fernandez, my fellow trainee puts it nicely as 'Some like Jack, some like Jill, but they like Jack and Jill'.

Training was tough, as expected in a boot-camp kind of a setup. Reveille was at 06:00 am followed by a health run and drill. After this, there would be classroom lectures classified as 'Education'. Flt Sgt Francis conducted these classes. We were not allowed to 'Book Out' of the camp during the initial training period.

Besides the four of us who had come from Poona, there were quite a few others who I made friends with. The most outstanding of them was PS Bhinder; a Sikh from Ludhiana. He was a natural leader and a bit of a maverick. He was later commissioned as a fighter pilot. Sohan Lal Tandon was another friend who was a handsome Punjabi – a physical fitness buff who was fond of having a full-fledged mustard oil bath on Sundays. He was commissioned as a transport pilot and used to fly Dakotas for many years. Bhaskaran was an ambitious and highly motivated youngster from Cannanore (an alumnus of Rajah's High School) who was also commissioned and became a navigator after winning the Sword of Honour from the flying Academy. Pakrasi, the senior man of the flight, a lanky footballer from Calcutta later represented the Air Force in football as the centre-forward. J Narayana Rao from Hyderabad was also a highly motivated person who showed intense interest in aeronautics and was the trainee Secretary of the Aero-Club formed under the aegis of Squadron Leader Gyani, who was the education officer of the unit. Rao's close friend Patni from Kumaon was from an army family who was later commissioned in the Kumaon Regiment.

One of the trainees was a chap named Gupta, who was desperate to get out of the Air Force as he realized quite early during the training programme that military life was not his cup of tea. He did considerable research on the subject of getting a discharge from Service and finally put in an application stating that one of his bachelor uncles who had immigrated to America and made good there had died leaving an amount of thirty million dollars to him and literally begged the Air Force authorities to release him. Surprisingly, his application went up through proper channels like a shot and he got his release within a month, proving that if you want your bluff to be believed, you must bluff big.

In our senior squadron, one Anglo-Indian boy named Rudy Hourigan gained fame as the all-India, all-Burma and all-Ceylon featherweight boxing champion. Two other contemporary boxers were Palfrey and MacDonald. MacDonald became a fighter pilot who was tragically killed in an aircraft accident. We used to watch these champions in action during the inter-unit boxing championships held on our campus, usually umpired by Flt Lt King Lee or Flt Lt Wakefield.

In September 1949, when we were half way through our training, I was told to report to Flt Lt Wakefield's office. When I reported to him, he put his arms round me and told me that there was a telegram for me conveying the sad news that my brother Ramdas had passed away. I was shocked at this news and insisted that I should be granted leave to attend the funeral in Chovva. He explained to me that it would be impossible for me to reach in time for the funeral and the rules did not allow the granting of leave while under training except under the most exceptional circumstances. Since my situation did not satisfy the Air Force's definition of most exceptional circumstance, my leave was regrettably denied. It took a while for me to get over this extremely distressing situation, but finally pragmatism prevailed and I reverted to normalcy.

We completed our training by the end of 1949 and I was given my choice of trade as Flight Mechanic (Engines) after matching my choice with the result of the PST Test. The passing-out parade was reviewed by Air Cmde RHD Singh, one of the five Air Commodores of the RIAF in 1949, who presented me a trophy for Best in Education.

My subsequent training would be at No. 2 Ground Training School at Tambaram in Madras. It would be for fifty-two weeks and would be commencing in January 1950.

My Brother Ramdas, 1948

My Brother Sathyapalan

Chapter 7

No. 2 Ground Training School Tambaram

The No. 2 Ground training school was located in Air Force Station, Tambaram, a distant suburb of Madras, close to the leafy environment of Madras Christian College. The Commanding Officer of the Station was Group Captain (Gp Capt) Rajaram, DFC, a fighter pilot who had distinguished himself at the Burma front during the Second World War. His brother Gp Capt Sitaram was also from the flying branch. The Officer Commanding the Ground Training School, Wing Commander (Wg Cdr) UK Nair, who had risen from the ranks as a Hawai Sepoy and was a vertically challenged shorty like me. In fact, he was shorter, being only about five-feet tall, but with a tough physique. Watching him in action, one got the feeling that smallness is a much unappreciated attribute in a human being! There was a joke going around among the trainees that if you find a flag car with nobody visible, you had better salute it, as Wingco would be in it.

We had to undergo a medical examination before the actual training commenced. Warren Tully, one of the trainees who was a practical joker, informed us who were awaiting our physical examination that the medical exam was a piece of cake as it involved only a simple procedure during which a doctor looked into one ear and another looked into the other ear, and if they could not see each other you were in and if they could see each other you joined the Air Force Police. He nearly got into trouble for divulging this piece of information but was saved as the medical sergeant who overheard this had a sense of humour.

On the first day of our training, Wg Cdr UK Nair addressed us and concluded by saying that success in life, as in the Air Force, was achievable by 99% perspiration and 1% inspiration.

We had some excellent Instructors for aero engines. Cpl Maximus taught us 'Preliminary Engines', which provided to be a solid base in aero-engine technology. Cpl Karunakaran was the instructor for the Gypsy Major engine fitted on the Tiger Moth Trainer. Cpl PD Nair taught us the nuts and bolts of Pratt and Whitney Twin Wasp engines which powered the Dakota aircraft. The more complicated Griffon Engine fitted on the Spitfire aircraft was taught by Sgt Menon and the Centaurus Engine, powering the Tempest by Sgt Phillip. The Hamilton Standard propellers and a couple of other types of propellers were the domain of Sgt Paddington (anglicized version of Padmanabhan). They were top class instructors highly trained in the methods of instruction and with a wealth of experience to back it up. I was keen to learn as much as I could about aero engines and the accessories fitted on them. The training was so good that we could dismantle the entire Hamilton Standard propeller and put it back together in half a day.

The engine section was under the overall charge of Warrant Officer Venkataraman, who was later commissioned and retired as a Squadron Leader. Sgt Paddington later became as a flight engineer and was selected as the flight engineer of the IL-14 aircraft presented by Marshal Bulganin to Pandit Nehru in 1955.

There was a cinema hall in the unit, which would screen English movies on most days with an occasional Hindi or other vernacular movies. I was a regular for English Western movies along with a Bangalore educated friend named Gajraj, who was from Madras but had his education in Baldwin School in Bangalore and spoke English with a fluent Anglo-accent.

On other evenings, some of us would retire to a study hall to gen up on training manuals.

An Anglo-Indian boy named George Foote taught me how to play the mouth organ. He was an excellent tap dancer and during the absence of the instructor in our classroom, he used to demonstrate tap dance numbers by doing it in the instructor's table but had to stop future demos as the instructor had returned early from his tea break and caught him in the act. Henry Fernandez, my old recruiting office friend was very good at singing mournful country and Western songs by Jim Reeves. He taught me the complete lyrics of a song called 'When it's lamp lighting time in the valley' by Norman Blake. I remember the song even after a lapse of sixty-five years.

These were the good parts of life in Tambaram. The bad parts included being cooped up and being allowed out only during weekends, when one could book out from the guardroom and walk down to Tambaram railway station, which was the terminus for the electric trains which ran at regular intervals from Tambaram to Park station in Madras city.

My classmate Dasaratha Ram Naidu had got admission for electrical engineering at the college of Engineering in Guindy. He later joined the Electricity Department of the Madras Electricity Department. I met him a couple of times at the College hostel and revived old memories.

We had to wear our uniform while going out and this rule was not particularly appreciated by the trainees, not because they were not proud of wearing it, but because it deprived them of their anonymity!

An aunt, Mrs Ananthalakshmi (my father's cousin) had an apartment in Adyar where she was living with her two sons and a daughter. She had married Mr Anantha Krishna Iyer, who was a professor in Rangoon University. She had settled down in Madras after he passed away, for the education of her children. One weekend, I paid her a surprise visit wearing my full uniform. She invited me to stay for lunch, which was very welcome after eating mess food for almost a year. After a post-prandial siesta, she regaled me with some interesting but hitherto unknown stories about some members of the Kunnathidathil family to which she and my father belonged. It appears that one of her brothers, Ramanunni, had gone away to Tibet as a jobless young man, moved to China and then disappeared till he surfaced in London. Many years later, he had a place in Sheppard's Bush, where he was staying with his English wife. He had a strange profession – he was an expert in manually gutting tennis rackets. In fact, it appears that he was so well known in the profession that many Wimbledon players were his customers. He had also changed his name to KR Menon, for unknown reasons.

Another interesting titbit she told me was that her sister Kanakamma was the wife of V Pangunni Menon (VP Menon) who was associated with Sardar Patel during the integration of Indian States. I had to leave before she could tell me more such stories of her family, as I had to get back before the booking in time of 23:59 hours. I promised to visit her again soon.

My brother Bharathan had completed his five-year course in automobile engineering from Ramakrishna Mission and had got a job in Bombay with Leyland Motors. But soon, he left Leyland and he joined Ford Motors where he was working while I was training at Tambaram. He used to visit my Adyar aunt during weekends while he was in Madras and stayed with them in Adyar off and on.

By the end of 1950, we completed our training and passed out as full-fledged technicians in different specialties known as trades. My trade was called Flight Mechanic Engines (FME). I got the Best Technician's trophy during the passing-out parade.

My posting orders were to No. 5 Heavy Bomber Squadron, Poona. The squadron was established with the Second World War vintage B-24 Liberator aircraft.

Best Technician Trophy, 1950

Flight Mechanics (Engines) 32nd Course No. 2 Ground Training School, 1951

Chapter 8

No. 5 Heavy Bomber Squadron Poona

I arrived at the Lohegaon base of Air Force Station Poona during the first half of January 1951. The squadron personnel were housed in billets located about a couple of kilometres from the squadron. The squadron, commanded by Wg. Cdr Akut (and later by Wg. Cdr Shipurkar), had twelve Liberators, divided equally between two flights, A Flight and B Flight. Each Flight had five B-24 of the Heavy Bomber version and one of the Cargo versions. I was allotted to the A Flight. The pilots in A Flight were Flt Lts Mehta, Grewal, Ghadiok, Agtey, Pushong, Dodsworth, Wordsworth, 'Satoo' Williams, Bakshi, Vohra and Paul who were all Flt Lt's and a few other junior officers who were co-pilots. The other officer crew were navigators, the names I recall being Fg Offr ST Nair, Chaabra, Dhige and Vir Narain. The flight engineers were Daruvalla, Mathews, Apte, Mukherjee, Abernathy and Paddington.

Flt Lt Paul and crew were the first from the Air Force to fly over Mt. Everest (in a Liberator of 102 Survey Flight) and they had taken a spectacular photograph of the pristine peak which was published in National Geographic magazine later. However, soon thereafter Paul crashed and died in a Liberator accident. It was said that he died as he had violated the sanctity of the holy Everest peak.

Bakshi was an outstanding field hockey player and had represented India in international matches and later in the Melbourne Olympics. Subsequently, he joined Air India which he left after a few years and joined Singapore Airlines.

Flt Lt Arnold Sachindranath Williams, popularly known as 'Satto' Williams, was an unusually interesting person and a fine gentleman – gentle in manners and gentle in his flying. But he did not stay long in the squadron. He opted out of Liberators and went on to fly helicopters. It was said that he could not operate the rudder pedals of the Liberators to their full range of movement as he was too short – about five feet four inches or so. The Bell helicopters he started flying had no such problem and hence he opted out from the big heavy bomber to the delightfully petite Bell choppers. He later won the Vir Chakra flying helicopters in 1962 when he was shot down by the Chinese while on a casualty evacuation sortie. Another version for his decision to opt out of Liberators was that he had embraced the Baha'i faith, which eschewed violence of any kind, and since a heavy bomber could not be considered non-violent; he decided to fly benign machines like helicopters.

The pilots and navigators were staying in a requisitioned building on the Poona–Ahmednagar highway known as the Aga Khan Palace which had been converted into the officers' mess. They used to commute to the squadron on powerful 5 HP motorcycles like Norton, AJS, BSA, Matchless' Honda, Yamaha and the 750 cc lquid cooled Harley Davidson. One of them used to own an American made Indian Chief which was the envy of all bike lovers.

In 1952, the pilots and navigators of the squadron decided to have moustache growing championship competition. The kick off date was1 Feb 1952, a few days after the republic day flypast in Delhi where the Libs had taken part. The competitors had to be clean shaven on the day of the kickoff and on Independence day some seven months later a panel of judges would announce the results based on the quality, the wingspan, colour and shape of the moustache. Flt. Lt Owen Derck Dodsworth ("Dodo") won the first prize with his golden brown, big and bushy Hungarian moustache. The runner up was Fg.Offr ST Nair, the smart, ebullient navigator who had grown an imperial moustache (Kaiser Wilhem style) very similar to what is known as the handle bar moustache.

The Liberators had a distinguished war record in the European, Mediterranean and in the China–India–Burma theatres. Incidentally, the famous Hollywood actor, James Stewart had taken part in the European sector as a B-24 Pilot. The ones being operated in No. 5 Squadron were from among the forty-two Liberators recovered and restored by Hindustan Aircraft Ltd from the aircraft salvage yard at Chakeri airfield in Kanpur. Most of them were ex-RAF, provided to them by the USA under the Lend-Lease programme and had been made deliberately unusable when the Allies left India, as per the Lend-Lease terms. Hindustan Aeronautics Limited (HAL), under the leadership of a technical wizard named Yellappa, made the aeroplanes fly worthy for a one-off sortie to Bangalore and they were ferried one by one by the redoubtable Chief Test Pilot of HAL, Captain 'Jimmy' Munshi.

Air Force Station Poona (No. 2 Wing) was commanded by Gp Capt Victor Srihari. Besides No. 5 Heavy Bomber Squadron, No. 3 squadron with Tempest aircraft under the command of Sqn Ldr McKenzie was operating from the other side of the runway.

I made a number of friends in the Squadron. There used to be many small groups formed based on shared interests. One such group included Saigal, Mukherjee, Kashmira Singh and Stanislaus (my old Madras recruiting office acquaintance). Another member of this smart group was Santanam who came to be known as Satan. Donald Kishander was a smart technician who later became a flight engineer. Saigal left the Air Force after nine years and later worked in the Sea Lord Restaurant in Connaught Place, Delhi. He later started his own restaurant in New Delhi, which grew into a chain with branches in Bombay as well. Mukherjee became a football star and was a part of the Air Force football team.

Another group was a very highly motivated one, totally devoted to advance their careers. One of them was SP Choudhry. He teamed up with Gera and started studying for the AMIE Examination. Later, both of them cleared the exams and Choudhry was commissioned in the Engineering Branch of the Air Force and Gera joined HAL as an engineer.

I too got interested and did some research of my own. The AMIE syllabus was not purely aeronautical in nature, which was what I was keen on. Then one day I saw a booklet published by the British Institute of Engineering Technology (BIET) based at Bombay, which was offering courses to prepare candidates for the Associate Fellowship Examination of the Royal Aeronautical Society, London. I got in touch with them and signed up for the course. The subjects chosen by me were Applied Mathematics, Aerodynamics, Theory of Prime Movers and Fuels, Aircraft Structures, Aircraft Design and Development and Aero-Engine Design.

Our routine involved daily inspection of the engines of the multi-engined Liberator, fitted with four Pratt & Whitney R1830-43 engines, almost similar to the P&W Twin Wasp engines fitted on the DC-3 Dakota aircraft. The main difference was that the engines on the Libs had turbo-superchargers. These were exhaust gas-driven turbines coupled to rotary air compressors, which would compress the air going into the engines, thereby utilizing the energy from the exhaust gases, which would otherwise be wasted. The daily inspection also involved opening the four fuel drain cocks to drain the water, which might have accumulated at the bottom of the four fuel tanks and wire-locking them afterwards. The propellers were also required to be manually turned through two revolutions to let the oil from the bottom cylinders of the engines to drain out into the manifold. The refuelling of the aircraft was also the engine technicians' responsibility. The aircraft fuel sight gauges showed the fuel contents in US Gallons, whereas the fuel supplied by the fuel bowsers was in imperial gallons. We got used to the simple conversions in a short time. After about six months experience, some of us were allowed to run up the engines to check various systems, particularly the mag drops (the drop in revolutions per minute (RPM) when each of the magnetos were switched off in turn). If this exceeded the specified amount, the rectification of the snag involved the laborious process of replacing either the seven front-row spark plugs or rear-row spark plugs. I had found a shortcut to this by physically feeling the spark plugs and replacing only the ones which were slightly colder to the touch compared to the others. One needed to do this as soon and the engines were switched off and one needed to have heat-sensitive fingers.

Each of us was allocated a specific aircraft (we used to call them kites), which gave us some pride of proprietorship. Flt Sgt Wig, a burly Punjabi, was the Chiefy of the flight. Chiefies were very powerful supervisors and had direct access to the squadron boss. There were other supervisors for each trade. The Engine Supervisor was Sgt Onkar Singh, a modified Sardar, who was an exceptionally proficient technical supervisor.

I had started my studies, and made full use of the spare time available to me when my allotted aircraft went in for Minor inspection or was unserviceable or on Aircraft on Ground (AOG) awaiting spare parts. These were usually made available by cannibalizing them from other aircraft, some of which became 'Christmas Trees', never going to fly again. I made use of these Christmas tree aircraft for my studies by making use of the navigator's seat and table in the aircraft.

Meanwhile, No. 3 squadron, located on the other side of the runway, suffered a series of fatal crashes, mostly due to engine failures. They had lost two commanding officers, Sqn Ldr Suri and Sqn Ldr Coelho earlier and subsequently during a short period the squadron lost Flt Lt Davis, Flt Lt Date,

Fg Offr Damle and Fg Offr D'Cruz; all their names starting with letter D. It appeared as if some kind of nemesis was attached to the names of these pilots. The frequent failures of the sleeve-valved Bristol Centaurus engines which powered the Tempests were the main causes of these fatal accidents.

We took part in many funeral parades on the bank of the Mutha-Moola River to bid our sad goodbyes to these young fighter pilots.

My older sister and brother-in-law with their baby boy had moved out to Madras to their new posting. My brother Bharathan who was working at Ford Motors in Bombay as a service engineer had lost his job as the American employers had closed their set-up in India soon after India had got independence. He managed to get a job in Poona as works manager of an automobile firm and was staying with a Parsi family as a paying guest. The Mistry family with whom he was staying were very fine, enlightened folks and I had spent many nice weekends with them. I would send half of my meagre salary to my mother. Things had improved quite a bit financially after the two of us started working. My sister Sarala had joined the Government Brennen College to do her Intermediate Science course. She was put in a ladies hostel run by a family staying close to the college and was quite happy there. My youngest brother Sathyan was in the final year at Chovva High School. He had an unusual pet, a jackal, which he had retrieved from our compound as a pup and was happily living in the house. But when he grew up, his genes took charge and he started eating up the neighbours' chickens.

We were permitted sixty days annual leave and twenty days casual leave every year. I gave up the casual leave and would take my full annual leave every year except in 1953 when the squadron had to go to Khambalia in Gujarat for the bombing trials at a range near Jamnagar. We lived in tents and under rather primitive living conditions in Khambalia, but the novelty compensated for all the trials and tribulations of the harsh life there. There was a detachment of No. 14 squadron with Spitfire MK 18 aircraft under the command of Sqn Ldr 'Ganja' Bose, who had also come there for gunnery trials. He used to punish young pilots who were not up to the mark by making them double up and down on the tarmac. I saw Plt Offr Bhadwar being given this disciplinary treatment once. He was an ex-TTC apprentice and had been commissioned after being posted to No. 5 squadron for a while.

In January 1954, we went to Delhi to take part in the Republic Day flypast – an annual event after 1950 when nine Liberators would fly past Kingsway (now renamed Rajpath).

On our return to Poona, I got my posting orders to No. 4 Equipment Depot located at Manauri, near Allahabad. This was a non-flying station, so I was not particularly happy about it. But this would give me time to concentrate on my studies.

My Brother Bharathan, 1955

Chapter 9

Air Force Station Manauri Allahabad

I arrived at No. 4 Equipment Depot (renamed No. 24 ED), located at Manauri, a suburb of Allahabad, in February 1954. This depot was established for the storage and pre-issue inspection of aircraft spare parts. An officer of the erstwhile Equipment Branch, now renamed the Logistics Branch, commanded the unit. Most of the officers and airmen of the unit were from the Equipment Branch/Trade. Since pre-inspection of aircraft spares were to be done before issue, a small element of technical personnel under a Chief Technical Officer was also established at the unit. These personnel were specially trained Aeronautical Inspection Service (AIS) specialists.

I reported to the chief technical officer (CTO), Flt Lt Ramappa of the Technical Engineering Branch. He was an old timer, marking time for superannuation. I was asked to work with a team who were tasked to overhaul a number of diesel generating sets which had been in storage since the war. They were brand new Mirlees Blackstone Gen Sets and we were given carte blanche to dismantle them to the crankshaft level, service them, re-assemble them and certify them as serviceable after running them till all electrical and mechanical parameters were satisfactory. It was a very satisfying job, engineering-wise. It also gave me plenty of spare time to pursue my studies. I had completed the syllabus for all four subjects of Part 1 of the Examination and wrote to the Royal Aeronautical Society at 4 Hamilton Place, London to schedule the dates for my examination. The examination was accordingly scheduled for 4th September 1955 and my Centre was the Central College, Bangalore. In fact that was the only centre in India.

My annual leave was granted and I proceeded to Bangalore and took a room in a lodge near the City Railway Station. There were six Air Force candidates appearing for the exam, one from HAL and four from Ceylon. I did quite well in all the four papers, particularly the paper on Aircraft Design and Development.

My mother and Sathyan had moved to Madras as Bharathan had got a job with Leyland Motors, Bombay as a Service Engineer. He had taken a small house on rent on Raja Rao Garden Street and used to commute on alternate weekends to Madras. Sarala had joined Presidency College, Madras, for her MSc in Chemistry after completing her BSc from Queen Mary's College. Sathyan had got admission to the Government Arts College, Madras for his Intermediate course. He was keen on getting a medical degree and had therefore taken the second group for his Intermediate course.

After my exam in Bangalore, I spent a quiet two months in Madras and concentrated on studying for the Part 2 subjects of the RAeS course.

On reaching Manauri after my annual leave, I was shocked to learn that Eustace Bayross, a happy go lucky boy from Ooty and an armament tradesman, had been awarded twenty-eight days detention for failing to account for two rounds of ammunition while he was on duty as duty armourer. He was a nice guy but very careless about things.

We had a reading room cum library in the unit known as the 'Information Room', which was a standard welfare measure in all Air Force Units. The person who was managing it was getting posted out to Kanpur and they were looking for a volunteer replacement. I promptly volunteered and was completely briefed by the incumbent, Harold Miranda. Harry was from a railway family. His father was an Engine Driver for South Indian Railways (SIR); on his retirement, he had got a lump sum amount which he had invested in a farmhouse in Yalagiri Hills near Jolarpet Railway Station. During my leave period, he had invited me to the farmhouse and I was quite fascinated by the place. So we had a good understanding with each other. He also managed to get me a room to stay attached to the Information Room. This was godsend for me, as I could prepare for my exam without any disturbance.

Another friend of mine was Shashi Bhaskaran, who was also from Cannanore. He was a well-read individual with an unusual interest in books on European mythology. He was the person who introduced me to beer. I shared my first bottle of beer with him one evening during which we decided to visit the city of Benares. Another friend, Sundara Rao, who was getting some help from me to pursue his studies for the AMIE Exam in Electrical Engineering, also wanted to join us for the trip to Benares. We took three days casual leave and boarded an overnight train to Benares, where we managed to get a room near one of the burning Ghats. All three of us were not particularly religious and were infrequent visitors to places of worship. But we found that this place vibrated with some kind of energy which was a fascinating experience. Next morning, we naturally gravitated to one of the burning Ghats and got a reality check when we saw the dead body of a woman floating peacefully in the Ganges. Before our immature minds could grasp the situation, folks around told us that it was the body of a postmaster's widow and it was customary for the tranquillity of the soul to consign the body to Mother Ganga. In memory of our visit to Benares, we took our group photograph from a photo studio in the vicinity.

We got back to Manauri and the very next evening we were taken in a three-tonner truck to witness a table tennis tournament at Allahabad University where one of our Air Force chaps was participating. His name was Elias and he was a bit of a champion and easily scored over the university champion.

I had meanwhile completed the syllabus for Part 2 of my exam and about a year after getting the pass result of Part 1 was ready to appear for the final exam. I managed to get my annual leave for 1956 and had to go to Bangalore for the exam. This time we were only three candidates. The paper on aero-engine design was of a type never seen before by any of the candidates. It had four questions with an array of elaborate data and the candidates were instructed to answer one or two questions fully. I thought I had done justice to the paper. Arriving back in Manauri in a relaxed frame of mind, I reset my priorities and started enjoying life a bit. One of my friends, AK Mehta started accompanying me on weekend liberty runs and we would visit Niranjan talkies located in the busy chowk area of Allahabad city. After the movie, we would invariably enjoy the culinary delights of the city and he introduced me to the first smoke of my life. The cigarette we tried was a perfumed one, the name of which I do not wish to recall.

There were a few other interesting characters I came to know subsequently. One was an account assistant named Poplee who had the looks of Rock Hudson. Out of uniform he was always nattily dressed and we heard later that he had joined Bollywood after leaving the Air Force. Another person who left an imprint on my memory was a chap named Tariang from the North-East who was very good ballroom dancer and would go out on weekends to the Allahabad Railway colony along with a couple of Anglo-Indian boys, of whom I remember Eddy Burrows and Rudy Miranda, the younger brother of

Harold Miranda. We had an outstanding basketball player on the unit strength, named John, who was on the Air Force basketball team.

My results came out a month later and I was declared successful and was now a graduate of the Royal Aeronautical Society, London, which was considered equivalent to a degree in aeronautical engineering – no doubt a backdoor entry but personally a very satisfying outcome. My boss, the newly posted Chief Technical Officer, Flt Lt Gupta personally took me to the commanding officer, who after congratulating me gave me the task of giving lectures to equipment officers who were mostly arts graduates to enable them to understand the fundamentals of aeronautics.

By the end of 1956, my posting orders had come for a flying unit temporarily formed at Kanpur exclusively for training Afghan pilots. The name of the unit was 105 Conversion Training Unit (105 CTU) and its officer commanding was a fighter pilot and a Qualified Flying Instructor, Flt Lt Yadav.

Chapter 10

105 Conversion Training Unit Kanpur

I arrived at Air Force Station, Chakeri, Kanpur to take over my new assignment. Air Force Station, Kanpur was a very large station. Headquarters Maintenance Command and No. 1 Base Repair Depot (BRD) were both located there.

Air Vice Marshal Harjinder Singh, the legendary engineer who joined the Air Force as a Hawai Sepoy and rose to be the Air Officer Commanding-in-Chief (AOC-in-C) of Maintenance Command located at Chakeri, Kanpur, is the name widely associated with Air Force Station, Kanpur. The stamp of his personality was evident in full measure on the first day of my arrival. Normally, the uniformed personnel of an Air Force Station go to work independently or are taken by Air Force vehicles depending on the distance to be covered. In Kanpur, all personnel had to congregate and form up in flights and squadrons and march to their respective sections/hangars to the accompaniment of a full-fledged band. This would be the protocol each and every working day. Even the civilian employees were part of the marching columns.

Our unit was located near the tarmac adjacent to the runway. We were established with Spitfire Mark nine trainers and Mark eighteen fighter aircraft. The trainer is powered by the Rolls Royce Merlin Engine and the fighter was fitted with the more powerful Griffon Engine. Both the engines were twelve-cylinder Vee engines and liquid cooled with a mixture ethylene glycol and water. The starting system was completely different from conventional electric starters. They were Coffman starters (known as shotgun starters) and used cartridges like in a twelve-bore gun. The gas from the cartridges when fired would rotate the crankshaft through powerful gearing.

The unit had to train three Afghan pilots. One of them, Pilot Officer Ahmed, was a temperamental type and one of the training sorties, the spitfire swung viciously on landing. When the instructor Flt Lt Yadav castigated him, he nearly became physically violent. That would have been the end of his career, but better sense prevailed on both sides and the matter was amicably resolved.

I made some good friends in Kanpur. Pranab Kumar Maitra was one of them. He was a bit of an intellectual type from Calcutta and his father was a senior engineer with Tatas in Jamshedpur. We would go every evening after a lousy dinner in the mess to have a nightcap of masala tea from the popular Bania shopwala.

He was well versed in Rabindra Sangeet and he taught one Bengali poem which I still remember. In Bengali it goes like this:

'Jadha Bhadohok Indra dhanushe

sudheer akasha anga

Ami bala basha more

Prajapatithir paaka'

On translation, it gives the following meaning:

'The rainbow in the sky is lovely and beautiful,

But I prefer by far the butterflies on my humble earth'

Pranab was a very sensitive guy and was fond of Bengali poetry and one of them translated to English was his contribution to my autograph book. It goes as follows:

'If I could love only

And not covet,

Nature would surely

For a moment

Smile softly and dearly

And wouldn't lament

Over my folly

For like any other being

I had no inkling,

And so I loved, coveted and lost;

But Oh Nature, show me a creature

That loves, but covets not'.

I lost track of this gentle and refined friend of mine after a while and despite many efforts to find him did not succeed. Friendships are vulnerable and so likely to disappear, overcome by space, time and one's own family life.

Another old friend I met in Kanpur was Achuthan Kutty Menon who was with me in Poona. He was from Calicut (Perumpilavil House, Mangav, Calicut) and we were in touch for a long time and then I lost track of him. I heard that after leaving the Air Force, he worked as an electrical engineer in the Andaman Islands.

John Godfred Benedict was another newfound friend. He had passed out as an apprentice from TTC as an Armament specialist and was a church-going Catholic. Originally from Mangalore, he had settled down in Puthiyara in Calicut and had a house right behind my cousin Dr VK Balraj's clinic.

There was another flamboyant character named David who, it appears, had also passed the AFRAeS Exam and after leaving the Air Force had started a business in Delhi along with an ex-Air Force colleague named Tilak Raj. I never heard of him after our stint in Kanpur.

Maintenance of the Spitfire aircraft was a bit of a tricky affair as the accessibility of engine parts was complicated. The engine panels were not fastened with Dzus fasteners like the Liberators and Dakotas, but with Amal fasteners and needed special tools to open and close them. The Coffman Starters were also not maintenance friendly. However, the propeller blades were made of laminated wood and if landings were messed up, which were common incidents with Ahmed and his co-Afghans, the blades used to just break off when the nose-heavy landings occurred, with no structural damage to the aeroplane. Changing the propeller blades was no big deal.

It was a great feeling to give a ground-run to a Spitfire, as the sheer power of the Griffon Engine was exhilarating and when it was slow-running, the ticking of the twelve-cylinder engine had a musical cadence to it. You have to hear it to believe it. Those who have heard the ticking of a 5 Horse Power four-stroke engine of a motorcycle would appreciate this.

In the evenings, the bar used to get very crowded and it looked as if there were real hard drinkers in the Station. Occasional fights used to break out and the Orderly Officer of the day would have to be called to restore order.

The BRD, being the largest BRD in the country, had a large number of hangers. The professionally most interesting one was the engine hanger where the Goblin Engine overhaul line had just been set up. The De Havilland Goblin engine was the latest engine in the Air Force's inventory and the Vampire aircraft on which the Goblin was fitted was the first jet aircraft in the IAF.

The rig room in the Engine hanger was the heart of the Goblin Overhaul line as the fuel pump calibration was being done here. One Technician named Elias was the kingpin in the rig room. Later, he was employed as Chief Supervisor at Hindustan Aircraft Limited's Bangalore Division.

The three Afghan pilots went for their solo without a hitch although in the case of one of them it was touch and go. Finally, the unit was wound up by the third quarter of 1957. All personnel of the unit were posted out to different units. My posting was to No. 12 Squadron in Agra, which was the largest transport base in the country at that time with C-119G Packet aircraft and C-47 Dakota aircraft operating from the base. No. 12 Squadron to which I was posted was equipped with the C 119G Packet aircraft in 'A' Flight and the C-47 Dakota aircraft in 'B' Flight.

Chapter 11

No. 12 Squadron Agra

I was a little intimidated on arrival at this very large flying station. But I soon got acclimatized to the atmosphere, which had a mix of Packet aircraft, Dakotas and Canberra medium bombers. The Packet crowd was a little uppity as they were regularly going on Courier trips to the UK and used to look down on the Dakota folks. One person named '12 Volts' Raghavan who was a regular UK courier guy brought me a Seiko wristwatch on his return from there.

The station was commanded by Wg Cdr Marathe. I do not recall who the Officer Commanding of No. 12 squadron was, but the flight commander of the Dakota Flight was Flt Lt KD Kanagat.

One morning, I saw the eagerly awaited ad in the *Hindustan Times* inviting applications for commissioning in the Engineering branch of the Air Force. As the age and qualifications matched, I applied through the proper channel. It went through the Engineering Officer and the Squadron Commander, both of whom recommended and forwarded it to the Station Commander. After a week, I was called for an interview with the Station Commander, who after 10 minutes of interviewing me rejected my application saying that I was too short to be a commissioned officer. My design flaw had again come in to thwart me. I was advised by my boss to put in for an interview with the AOC-in-C. But meanwhile the last day for the receipt of the application was rapidly approaching, and by the time my application was routed through to the proper channel it was too late. I would therefore have to try my luck outside the Air Force as my term of engagement was soon coming to an end.

A few days after my rejection, the Dakota flight of the squadron had to go on a detachment to Srinagar. I was also a member of the detachment ground crew. Life in Srinagar was a different experience altogether. Work on the Dakota was much simpler after my experience on the Liberators and Spitfires, the only difference being that every morning as part of the daily routine, the aircraft had to do what is known as tail-up taxiing, which involved the aircraft being taken to the runway where the pilot had to carry out the first part of a take-off run, getting its tail up and then slowing down until the tail would come down. The aircraft would then be taxied back to the tarmac. The reason for this was to get any water accumulation at the rear end of the fuel tanks to get trapped in the sump of the fuel tanks from where they could be drained by opening the fuel cocks. The pilots were not happy to do this and the junior pilots were given this unpopular task.

The Dakota's primary task was supplying the troops located in the forward areas of Jammu and Kashmir. Some of these missions were landing sorties to Leh and some to the Advance Landing Grounds (ALGs). Others were dropping sorties in which supplies were dropped by parachute. A few aircraft were modified for the dropping sorties by removing part of the door on the left side of the fuselage. The dropping load would be lashed on special palettes and placed on rollers and literally pushed out by the trained loadmasters who were the Army ASC jawans. Occasionally, the dropping load consisted of live goats known as 'meat on the hoof'. This ensured that the soldiers on duty at the snow-bound borders were provided with the stipulated protein diet. Alcoholic nourishment for these folks was also dropped in the form of rum bottles on specially designed palettes.

The life of the Dakota crew at Srinagar has been poignantly portrayed in the following few lines:

'At dawn, the Dak with destination known
Beyond the clouds and mists of clinging grey
Await with pregnant load, ready to be flown
To Kargil, Rajouri or maybe to Leh
It seems so long ago that I crept along
Through dismal rain and darkness on the ground
At Srinagar, where winter nights are long
To drain the cocks and turn the props around
It is as if a tapestry is unfurled
Of mem'ry such as holds my soul content
If now perchance I'm abruptly hurled
Backwards in time, there shall be no lament'.

Srinagar was a delight in winter. A canopy of snow covered the roofs of the buildings and barracks. The wings of the aircraft would also be completely covered in snow which would have to be cleaned before the aircraft could be readied to fly, weather permitting. The pilots and navigators would also join up cheerfully along with the ground crew to clear the snow.

On weekends, a trip to town with visits to the Shalimar gardens and a stroll along the bank of the Jhelum, with vendors selling freshly fried trout, and a shikara ride in the Dal Lake were the kind of memories which we would treasure for years to come.

I was keen to appear for the Aircraft Maintenance Engineer's License (C License) examination for P&W Series engines, for which I had the Directorate General of Civil Aviation (DGCA) mandated experience on type and had applied to sit for the exam in Delhi the coming week. I applied for five days casual leave and was hoping to go in one of our Dakota's going to Agra for minor inspection via Delhi. This exam would have made the change in my career into civil aviation much easier when my term in the Air Force would end in July 1958, in just a few months. However, the detachment commander turned down my leave. I had an interview with him and he told me that service came first and I was required to proceed to Leh for an engine change for a Dakota which had got stuck there due to an engine failure. I felt completely dejected at my sheer sense of powerlessness in the presence of authority. But the feeling eventually got refracted by the passage of time. With the luxury of retrospective wisdom, I suppose it was for my own good that it happened the way it did.

The engine change at Leh took longer than expected due to heavy snowfall. We then flew back to Srinagar in the same engine-changed aircraft.

I had made some new friends in Srinagar. One was a chap from Mangalore named Rao who had been in the squadron for three years and would always volunteer for Srinagar detachments and had been my mentor and guide for enjoying the delights of Kashmir. Normally, the detachment would move to Jammu during the winter, but this year winter had set in early. So we moved to Jammu a week earlier than usual.

Jammu was warmer than Srinagar. I met a relative by marriage, one Balakrishnan from Cannanore who had been posted to the Station a couple of years earlier. He introduced me to a Kerala restaurant in town, which we started visiting on weekends for fish curry and rice lunches, a welcome change from mess food.

After a few months in Jammu, I got orders from the squadron to get back to Agra for my final clearance, as my term of service was coming to an end in July 1958.

At Agra, I finished all the clearances in a week time and during the next week made visits to the Taj Mahal, Agra Fort and some other touristy places, as I believed that I might not have a chance to see these places again. How wrong I was!

Some friends gave me a beer and biryani farewell party, during which I had my second bottle of beer after joining the Air Force. They gave me a fond send-off from Agra city railway station on 14 July 1958.

The Air Force had given me a tremendous amount of professional experience and remarkable camaraderie, both of which were irreplaceable.

Chapter 12

Unemployed

After bidding goodbye to the Air Force, where I had joined as a teenager, it was as if an umbilical cord had been cut when I left. The excellence of the training, both military and professional, and the opportunity to work on aircraft like the B-24 Heavy Bomber, the Super Marine Spitfire and the venerable work horse, the C-47 Dakota, in addition to the opportunity to obtain a degree in aeronautical engineering – these were enough compensations for me for having been denied higher education in a formal university.

My family meanwhile had an incremental addition to their standard of living. Bharathan had got a promotion and had become the senior service engineer at Ashok Leyland Ltd, located at Ennore, a suburb of Madras. Sarala had passed her MSc in Chemistry with a First Class and had got a job as a lecturer in Seethalakshmi Ramaswamy College at Trichinopoly. Sathyan had joined Madras Medical College for his MBBS. The family had moved to a bigger house at Lawyer Jaganath Street at Guindy. This is where I landed up as an unemployed twenty-seven-year-old ex-Air Force veteran.

I looked around at the various options available to me. Civil aviation was not an option without an aircraft maintenance engineer (AME) License, which I had missed by a whisker. The only aeronautical options were HAL at Bangalore or becoming an instructor at either the Madras Institute of Technology at Chromepet or at either of the two AME Training Institutes which were up and running at the time. These were the Hindustan Institute of Engineering Technology at St Thomas Mount, Madras, owned by Mr Varghese, and the Southern College of Engineering and Technology at Chalakudy in Kerala, owned by Mr Luiz. I got a letter from an old friend from my Manauri days named Kotnis (a nephew of Dr Kotnis who became a legend as a volunteer doctor in China), a bright, eccentric character who had joined the Air Force in a moment of pique. He had got a job in the Chalakudi College after leaving the Air Force and informed me of a vacancy in the College.

While I was mulling over these options, two advertisements appeared in the newspapers one after the other, one asking for applications for flight engineers in Indian Airlines and the other for commissions in the Engineering Branch of the IAF. One of the residents in Lawyer Jaganath Street, Mr Chatterjee, was a flight engineer in Indian Airlines, and I used to watch him in his white uniform with three stripes on his shoulder being picked up by the airlines car whenever he was on duty and being dropped back after his flight duty was over. On one of his off days, I ventured to ask his advice about my chances of being selected for the flight engineer's job. He told me that very few flight engineers at that time were graduate engineers, but mostly ex-AMEs from within the airline itself and that considering my age, experience and qualifications, I stood a very good chance of getting selected. I thought about this for a couple of days and took a final decision. Based on age limit, this was the last chance for me to get a commission, and as I had an intense desire to wear the Air force uniform again, I applied for the Air Force directly, without going through the 'proper channel'.

After a couple of weeks, I got a registered letter from Air Headquarters, saying that my application had been accepted and that I would have to proceed to Dehra Doon to appear before the Services Selection Board (SSB) on 20 October 1958.

This was great news for me. As the day for my departure approached, I made a quick visit to Calicut and Chovva to visit my relatives at Ganesh Nivas and my folks at Ananda Sadanam. My uncles had passed away and my cousins had got married and were away in different places.

I returned to Madras after a few days and got ready to go to the SSB in Dehra Dun. I arrived on 19th October and met a few chaps who had also come from Madras. We were met at the station by a representative of the selection board and taken to the accommodation arranged for us near the Candidates' Mess. The next day, the President of the Selection Board briefed us. He explained the details of the selection process. It would be a 5-day programme; the first day would be a screening test; the second day we would go through psychological tests. On the third and fourth day, there would be a series of individual and group leadership tests, including a group discussion.

The tests were designed to evaluate the candidate's decision-making ability under stress, reasoning ability, ability to organize, communication skills, courage, self-confidence, determination, willingness to set an example and decision-making speed. Most of the tests needed average intelligence. While the tests were going on, besides the Group Testing Officer (GTO) who was actually the conductor, there were two or sometimes three individuals in civilian clothes taking notes silently. This was a bit off-putting to some of the candidates.

Besides the formal testing protocol, the candidates were also under observation as to how they conducted themselves during the course of their stay at SSB, where they were billeted for that duration.

We were divided into four groups of six candidates, each under the charge of a GTO. The GTO of my group was Sqn Ldr Ken Larkins. Each of us was allotted a chest number, to be worn throughout the duration of the test. We were required to address each other by the chest number and not by name. The GTO would also address us only by chest number.

I got a feeling that I had gone through the tests fairly well. However, during one of the group tests where I had to take a leadership role, I determined that the task would be impossible to carry out without violating one of the conditions imposed by the GTO. I decided to violate that condition and completed the task within the stipulated time. The other candidates in the group told me later that I had bungled by doing so and should have abandoned the task as impossible and that it would therefore adversely affect my grading. In the event, this actually went in my favour, which was confirmed the next day when the results were declared, chest number wise, by the President of the Selection Board. I found myself one among the four candidates selected out of the twenty-four.

After the other formalities were over, some of us made a quick visit to Mussourie, the neighbouring hill station and had a good time at the Mall.

The four of us who were selected were asked to report for our medical examination at the Central Medical Board (CMB), located at the Wellington Camp in New Delhi. I took a train to Delhi the next morning and stayed with an old friend who was in No. 5 Squadron with me, who after getting an AME license was working as an engineer with Indian Airlines and was staying in Lodi Colony with his brother.

The next morning, I reported to the CMB at Wellington Camp, commanded by Wg Cdr Jones. After the preliminary checks conducted by medical assistants and the other medical tests conducted by junior medical officers, Wg Cdr Jones, who happened to be an eye specialist conducted my eye test. He checked and rechecked my eyes and told me that my eyes had a rare asymmetric muscular peculiarity. However, he assured me it was not a defect and that he would clear me.

We were told to wait in the waiting room. After an hour or so, the adjutant came and announced that three of us had been cleared and that I was to report to the Commanding Officer, Wg Cdr Jones at 12:00 hours sharp. When I went to his office at noon, he informed me that I had been rejected as my height was below standard by three-fourth of an inch. However, this decision of the Board could be appealed to Air Headquarters. I would have to pay an appeal fee of Rs 40 to the treasury and appeal within a week. The adjutant was good enough to help me to fill the appeal form on the spot. The next day, I managed to pay the appeal fee and sent the appeal to Air Headquarters.

I reached home a bit crestfallen, despite the assurance given by Wg Cdr Jones that the appeal would be upheld. He would know, as there must have been precedents he was aware of. But this was small consolation when there could be many a slip between the cup and the lip.

But I need not have worried. I got a telegram from Air Headquarters after a week informing me that my appeal had been upheld, and that I had been selected for training at Air Force Technical College (AFTC), Jalahalli, Bangalore for the 15th Direct Entry Officers (DEOs) Course in the Technical Engineering Branch, commencing on 24 November 1958 and that detailed joining instructions were in post.

Air Force Selection Board, Dehra Dun, 1958

Chapter 13

Air Force Technical College Bangalore

I arrived at Bangalore City Railway station with all the stuff required to be brought as per the joining instructions, including a large black trunk of the dimensions specified. We were met at the station by a rep from AFTC and taken to Jalahalli.

The AFTC was founded on 4 July 1949 in collaboration with Air Service Training Co, Ltd, Hamble, UK, with Gp Capt J Beaumont MBE, DFC as its first Commandant. It was then called Technical Training College and got its present name on 1 January 1957, with Gp Capt MJ Kripalani, MBE as its first Indian Commandant. He would be our commandant during our training period of seventy-two weeks.

We were initiated into the Air Force in the conventional manner of initiation by ragging by our seniors of fourteen DEOs course (six months senior to us). This went on for a week without any serious issues.

As the course comprised of graduate engineers, we were granted commissions as Pilot Officers from the date of commission itself – that is, 24 November 1958. On the day of successful completion of the course, seventy-two weeks later, we would be granted an antedate of commission of two years, which would make the effective date of commission as 1 March 1958. We started wearing the stripes of a Pilot Officer on 24 November 1958, the day of the course commencement. There were a few selected senior non-commissioned officers (NCOs) who had joined the course who would be actually commissioned only on successful completion of the course. During the training period, they had to wear white shoulder patches and they were designated as Flight Cadets.

There were twenty-four of us in our course, which had four sub-branches. The Technical Engineering branch, to which I belonged, had seven DEOs and two flight cadets. The Technical Signals branch had four Direct Entry and five flight cadets. The Technical Armament branch had four Direct Entry and no flight cadets and the Technical Electrical had one direct entry and one flight cadet.

There were also three officers from the Indonesian Air Force who would be doing the course with us.

The course had two elements: the General Service element and the Engineering element. The General Service element comprised of Parade, Physical Training and Armament handling including the firing of weapons, games and lectures on service subjects. The Engineering element comprised of lectures on Basic Workshop, Aircraft Propulsion, Aerodynamics, Aircraft Structures, Metallurgy and Mechanical Transport. The practical part comprised of Aero Engines, Airframes, Electrics and Aircraft Instrumentation and finally the Flight Hangar including test bed familiarization.

Wg Cdr 'Lord' Ghosh, an officer of the GD (Nav) Branch, headed the GST Department. He was a flamboyant character and used to terrorize the trainees. The three officers under him were Sqn Ldr Sandison, Flt Lt Kundu and Pilot Officer ARS Murthy, all from the Administrative Branch (A&SD). Sandison was an exceptional instructor, a charming person with an impressive bearing. Murthy was a freshly minted officer just passed out from Air Force Admin College who initially had problems dealing with our trainees who would be senior to him in service.

The NCOs in the GST Section were top of the line drill instructors, particularly, Flt Sgt Chandran, who was always impeccably turned out and a typical Regimental Sergeant major type of martinet.

The Chief Instructor of the College was Wg. Cdr EK Nayanar, an avuncular officer of the Electrical branch. The instructor in the aeronautical department was Sqn Ldr Mukherjee, who headed the department. Aircraft Propulsion was taught by Flt Lt Godbole, Aircraft Structures and Metallurgy by Professor Vasavada, who had a PhD from MIT, USA. The other instructors were Flt Lt ND Mohan, Flt Lt SN Tyagi, Flt Lt AK Rangaraj, Flt Lt NR Rangarajan and Fg Offr SS Paul.

In my class, we had some bright engineers – R Ramamurthy with a first-class degree in Mechanical Engineering from Guindy Engineering College and S Kalayanasunadaram from Annamalai University. SS Bindra had left his graduate apprenticeship half way through from a Public Sector Company in Bihar and Parameshwaran from Bihar Institute of Technology. Mohan Raj had left a well-paying job with Standard Vacuum Oil Company (SVOC) to join the Air Force. Flt Cdt AI Washington was a happy go lucky Anglo-Indian Ex-Warrant Officer and Flt Cdt Mohan was also an ex-Warrant Officer who was a father figure for all of us; in fact, we addressed him as 'daddy-o'.

The Signals branch had RP Misra, a bright Electronics engineer who later on was sent by the Air Force to College of Aeronautics at Cranfield University, UK. MC Uthaya and KJ Hegde were some of the others in the course. Hegde was appointed as the Senior Man of our course. The Armament branch had three Indonesian Officers along with four Indian trainees, whereas the electrical branch had just one DEO and one flight cadet on the course.

The academic part of the course was a bit difficult for the two flight cadets, Washington and Mohan, but in the final academic exams after five months they managed to scrape through with tutorial help from some of us. However, two signal officers from our senior course did not make the grade in their final exams and were therefore back-phased to our course.

We had two projects to complete before the end of the course. One involved the design of a basic glider and its subsequent construction. The other was an individual project for which we had to select a topic for a thesis on an aeronautical subject, which would have to be approved by the department chief. I selected 'Boundary Layer Control' as the subject of my thesis, which was approved. I started working on it immediately.

We had a short break after the Final Academics and I went home to Madras and had a relaxed fortnight there. Sarala had got a job in SIET Women's' College as a Chemistry lecturer and she therefore had resigned from the college in Trichy. Sathyan was doing well at Madras Medical College and had passed his first year exam.

The second session of the training at AFTC was quite relaxing for me as it was all about specific engines with which I was quite familiar except for the Goblin turbojet Engine which was new to me. Every weekend, we would go out to town wearing our going-out dress: white shirt and white pant with Air Force tie. Our regular haunts were Koshy's Restaurant on Brigade Road for dosa and coffee, followed by a movie either at Regal Cinema or Rex Cinema and finally a meal at Continental Chinese restaurant on Brigade Road. There was another restaurant, which came up later called Blue Fox on MG Road.

Our seniors had introduced us to a ballroom dancing school called Snow's Dancing School, on Richmond Road. Some of us joined it and we learnt the rudiments of the Waltz, the Foxtrot and the Quickstep. One of my course mates wanted to learn the Tango as well, but gave it up later for reasons unknown. Mr Snow was of French–British origin and he had two middle-aged Anglo-Indian ladies as his assistant instructors and an old gramophone for the music. By the end of the course, we had some working knowledge of the three dancing disciplines. Any gaps in our technique were refined by our course mates, Mohan Raj and Kalyan, who were accomplished dancers even before joining the Air Force.

On weekdays, we learnt to play tennis. Mr Rakhra, who had a sports store on commercial street, was a regular visitor to the college and had supplied us with tennis rackets. By the end of the course, I could play a fairly good game of tennis. Frederick Jesuratnam, one of my course mates, who was a champion tennis player of Voorhees College, Vellore, was our teacher and coach.

We had what was known as Dining in Nights in the Mess once a month, which were very formal affairs for which we had to dress up in formal DJ's (stitched by Officers Wear Depot of MG Road – they made all our uniforms and lounge suits). At these dining in nights, all of us would have to get up and toast the President of India. The ritual was that at the end of the meal when the tables had been cleared and the waiters had withdrawn, the President of the dining-in-night, usually a staff member, would stand up and raising his wine glass (filled with water, not wine!) would announce 'Mr Vice, the President' and then the Vice-President of the dining-in-night, usually a trainee officer (all trainee officers had to do this in turn) would also stand up and say, 'Gentleman, The President', and then everyone would stand up and raise their glasses and toast the President. After this ritual was over, smokers could light up their cigarettes. Then, the President would pick the name of a trainee officer at random from a box, who would be asked to give a 5-minute extempore speech on a subject which would also be picked up from a box full of slips with subjects typed on them.

As the training was coming to a close, we started training for the passing-out parade. We were told that the parade would have to be perfect as the reviewing officer would be the Defence Minister of India, the redoubtable Mr Krishna Menon. Various levels of the college hierarchy supervised the practice parade and the prize winners were told to practice receiving the trophy and the entire routine had to be repeated till the commandant was fully satisfied.

The passing-out parade finally arrived. Pilot Officer KJ Hegde commanded it and everything went off well. Pilot Officer Mishra got the trophy for best in Signals, Flt Cdt Chandran for Electrical, Lt Subhagio for Armamant and I got the trophies for best in Engineering, Best in GST and the President's Trophy for the best all-round officer of the course.

It was customary to have a sit-down lunch with the reviewing officer of the parade, along with the staff and the passed out officers. It was a formal affair with the reviewing officer at the centre of the head table, the AOC-in-C Training Command,. Air Vice Marshal Ranjan Datt on his left and the best all-round officer on his right. We took our seats according to the seating plan displayed on the mess notice board. The Commandant escorted the Defence Minister to his seat. I was a bit nervous initially for being seated so close to this reputedly cantankerous dignitary, but he soon put me at ease by asking me where I was from and where I had studied. I had asked the headwaiter Jacob to serve me vegetarian food, as I was aware of the Defence Minister's food habits. Despite an elaborate menu which was displayed on the menu card at each place setting, he had only a bowl of yoghurt and three cups of tea. After lunch, he obliged me by signing on my copy of the menu card.

Well, that was the end of our seventy-two-week training course. My posting orders had arrived. It was to No. 101 Fighter Reconnaissance squadron, located in a place called Tezpur.

Before leaving, I was summoned to the Commandant's office where he presented me with a prize for the Best Thesis in the presence of the officer who had evaluated my thesis subject – Sqn Ldr S Radhakrishnan, an officer who had joined the Air Force in the Education Branch, despite having an engineering degree and who later was sent by the Air Force to the College of Aeronautics, Cranfield for post-graduation in aerodynamics. The prize was a book entitled 'Guided Weapons', which the Commandant told me seemed appropriate since I was getting posted to a fighter squadron.

No. 15 Direct Entry Officers Course, 1958

Defence Minister Mr Krishna Menon presenting the Best All-Round Officer Trophy, AFTC, 1960

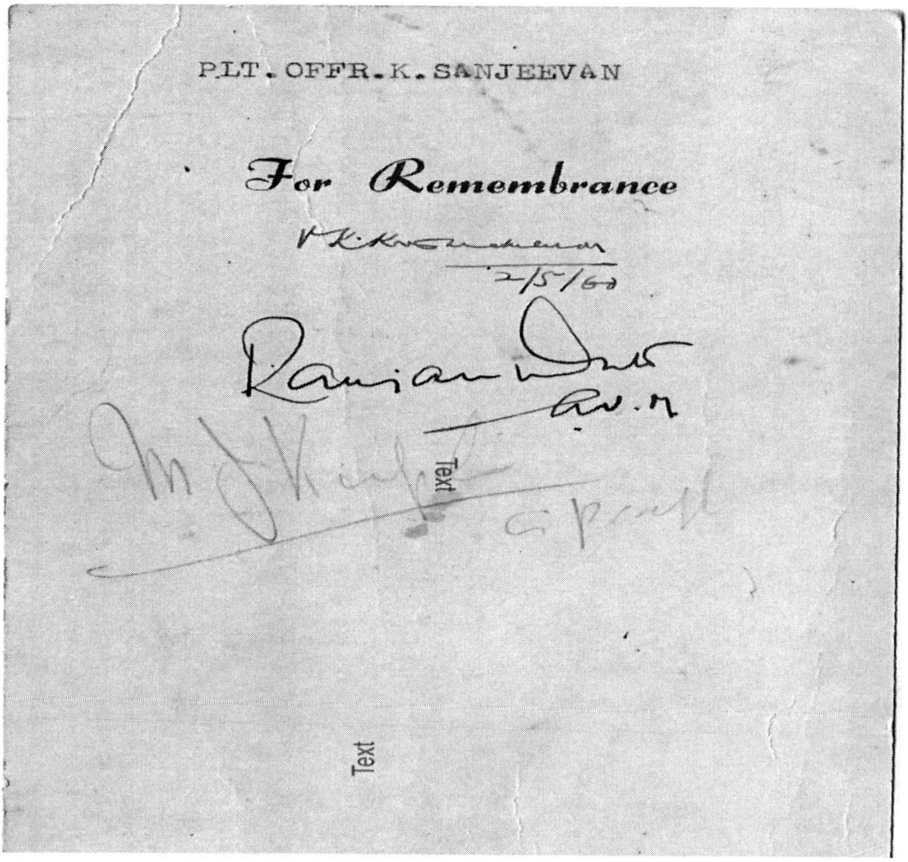

15 DEO Passing-Out Parade Lunch Menu Card,
signed by Krishna Menon, 1960

Chapter 14

No. 101 Fighter Reconnaissance Squadron Tezpur

I reached Tezpur after a long train journey via Calcutta and Rangiya. The accommodation was rather primitive. I had to share a bamboo hut called a Basha along with a pilot, Fg Offr Doraiswamy, ex-NDA, who became my philosopher, friend and guide, so to speak, during my breaking-in period in the squadron.

Tezpur is located on the Northern bank of the Brahmaputra River in the state of Assam. The airport known as Salonibari airport was constructed in 1942 by the RIAF. During the Second World War, the B-24 Liberators of the USAAF were based here. From 1959 onwards, the IAF started operations from there with two squadrons, No. 101 Fighter Reconnaissance Squadron with T-55 Vampires and No. 4 Squadron with Toofani Aircraft (Dassault Ouragan).

The base, known as No. 11 Wing, was commanded by Wg. Cdr 'Ganja' Bose, an outstanding Spitfire pilot and a man of tremendous energy. The No. 4 Squadron commander was Sqn Ldr Aubrey Michael, a quiet, gentle fighter pilot ('the more he heard, the less he spoke').

The officer commanding No. 101 Squadron, Sqn Ldr Lionel Cyprian Stephen (known as 'Chindy' Stephen) was a tough, pipe-smoking fighter pilot with whisky-soaked vocal chords. During my first meeting with him on my reporting to the squadron, he told me to get a flying overall issued and for the first month of my stay to fly in the right-hand seat of the two-seater Vampire T-55, and to start working as the squadron Engineer officer only after getting 25 hours of flying experience. The first sortie was with Flight Commander Flt Lt Sudarashan Handa. He asked me whether I had flown before and he was a bit surprised when I told him I had flown in a Lib, a Dak, a Harvard T6G and in a Spit trainer. He took me up to 20,000 feet and executed a loop and then a couple of barrel rolls, at the end of which I threw up into the oxygen mask that I had borrowed from Fg Offr Doraiswamy.

After landing, he went away without a word. I had to retrieve my manhood and so, without mentioning it to anybody, I got the mask replaced using the help of a young logistic officer, Plt Offr Rao.

I managed to get my CO's orders about getting 25 hours of flying experience executed before the month was out. But during one of the sorties with my roommate Doru, who was taking up the aircraft for a non-aerobatic, drop tank feed-test sortie, he asked me to put the pressurization on as soon as we took off. I asked him how and he told me to pull up the lever between the seats. I pulled up the lever and jettisoned the drop tanks! Apparently, the two levers were side by side and I had pulled up the wrong lever. Doru did not lose his cool and after flying around a bit he landed back and told me to sort out the mess I had landed both of us in. Cpl Verma, the technician who had installed the drop tanks asked me what we had done with them. I took him into confidence and told him what had happened. He had a solution. We went to see whether the OC's jeep was around. The driver told us that the boss had gone up for a long sortie. We took the jeep and drove through the over-run end of the runway, through the elephant grass, and found both the drop tanks lying within a hundred yards of each other, apparently undamaged. The tall elephant grass and the aerodynamics of the tank design had saved the situation. Verma, who was a physical fitness freak, loaded the tanks in the jeep and we drove to the station workshop, did a quick inspection for any damage, removed some scratches, carried out a quick leak test and were back near the aircraft in a jiffy. The tanks were fitted back well before the boss landed. Thank God for the elephant grass and the designers of the De Havilland drop tanks!

Among the other pilots in 101 were De Silva, NM Patel, Khullar, 'Dopey' Rao, Mullick, Tushar Sen, Brian De Magrey and a couple of others. The Squadron Doc was Flt Lt Ashish Roy, known as 'Kutha Roy' as he had an Alsatian as his pet. He was later known as a marathon runner of repute and had even taken part in the Boston Marathon when he was seventy years old. We had a photo interpreter, Fg Offr Ranganatha, who was working as the station adjutant as we did not have a full-time job of photo interpretation in the squadron.

Sqn Ldr D'Worsop was the Senior Medical Officer of the Station. His hobby was the nocturnal shooting of bats. I used to volunteer to assist him in this strange hobby, as he needed help in retrieving the bats he had shot.

He would quickly skin and cook the bats and eat them, as he believed that bat meat was good for health, especially for those afflicted with whooping cough. Nobody joined him in sharing this culinary delight, as none had the slightest signs of whooping cough.

Another officer of the Station was 'Doug' Venner who was D' Worsop's drinking companion. Both of them were jovial characters and were Falstaffian in their mannerisms and their girth.

Almost every day our boss would require all his boys to congregate in the bar for a drink or two. Absentees were considered anti-social. Often, a couple of drinks would extend till bar closing time, which the boss would extend as he, being the President of the Mess Committee (PMC), could do as he damn well pleased. On weekends, he would take all of us to the Thakur Bari club for an evening of dining and drinking with the local tea planters.

No. 4 Squadron folks were flying the more modern Toofani aircraft (the French Dassault Ouragan). They had Flt Lt Denzil Keelor as their Flight Commander, a man of tremendous energy and enthusiasm. He used to fly two sorties almost every day and play a game of hockey in the evenings with the airmen. Some of the others in the squadron were Flt Lt Godfrey Salins, Flt Lt Kashikar, Fg Offrs Kahai, 'Rondy Raina', Ronny Mitra, Bhupinder Singh and JP Singh. The Engineering Officer was Flt Lt Nissar Husain, a pipe-smoking officer with a regal bearing, educated in England and a fine gentleman. Since he was the senior most officer after the CO, whenever the CO went outstation on duty or leave, we would exchange positions and I would be attached as EO of No. 4 and he would take over my job as EO of No. 101, because only a pilot could take over as officiating OC and he could not serve under Keelor who would be officiating CO as Keelor was junior to him. This enabled me to get some experience on the Toofani aircraft and the Rolls Royce Nene engine fitted on it. After six months in the squadron, I was detailed to undergo a month's course on Fuel Quality Control Course conducted by SVOC in Bombay.

A week later, I was in Bombay at Cotton Green Air Force Mess. A couple of my course mates had also come for the course. Captain Manilal, a senior executive of the company, conducted the course at SVOC's facility at Wadala. When I got back in Tezpur, I was asked to give a lecture to the pilots of both squadrons about what I had learnt during the course.

Since we were in what is known as a forward area with a 56 Army Post Office (APO) address, all outgoing private letters were to be censored, self-censored by the officers and by the designated officers for airmen and NCOs. I was the designated censor officer for letters written in Malayalam. As a very large number of airmen in the squadron were Malayalees, I had a heavy job going through the letters, some of which used some colourful language not necessarily prohibited censorship-wise. I remember one case where an engine fitter of No. 4 squadron had written to his wife that he was living in a hut in the 'arse-end of Assam': it was more colourful in the vernacular. The prohibited portions, which included the location of units, aircraft types, etc. as laid down in the censorship regulations, were to be blackened out by the censoring officer, who was required to reseal the letter and stamp it with word 'Censored'.

One of the routine duties, which all junior officers had to do in turn, was Cipher duty. Any signal with the security classification 'Secret' and above would have to be in encrypted form. To receive such messages, they would have to be de-cyphered which was the duty of the cipher officer on duty. The messages could be either through the Book Cipher or the Machine Cipher. Some of the youngsters were not very happy doing cipher duties. I used to volunteer if any of them wanted to evade this duty. Instead, they would swap my orderly officer's duty with their cipher duty. For me it was a fascinating chore to see meaningless words and numbers forming themselves into words and sentences which made sense.

The Officers' Mess was run by the mess secretary assisted by different members like the treasurer, food member, bar member and the property member who were all appointed for specific terms. I was appointed as the library member soon after I arrived. The nucleus of the library was created by donation of books by the officers. Since these were too small in number, I was asked by my CO, which was also the PMC, to go to Calcutta by hitching a ride in a Dakota and buy a hundred books and come back in the same aircraft. I liked this assignment and went in the next Dakota courier aircraft to Calcutta, where I visited a large bookshop in College Street and selected a hundred books. As I had been given carte blanche to select any fiction books within the total budget, I bought all the PG Wodehouse books available and a few whodunits.

When I got back, the PMC had changed and Aubrey Michael had taken over. He happened to be a Jeeves fan and was delighted with my selection, and from then onwards he used to shorten my name to 'Jeeves'. This nickname got stuck as my moniker permanently.

One of the serious problems plaguing the vampire fleet was the frequent malfunctioning of the Goblin engines due to rear bearing failures. A method had been developed to monitor the health of the rear bearing by measuring the run-down time of the engine, which involved measuring the time taken by the engine to come to a complete stop after the engine had been switched off. A record of this was maintained and based on this, one could assess the health of the rear bearing and withdraw the engine from service if it turned really nasty. This gave me plenty of opportunity to run up the engine frequently and become intimate with the aircraft.

I had hardly worked in the squadron for eighteen months when my posting orders arrived to the AFTC, Bangalore, as an Instructor. I handed over charge to my successor, Pilot Officer CO Shah, who was two courses junior to me. I had meanwhile got promoted to Fg Offrs rank and had been given two medals, despite the fact that I had not fought in any war nor got any gallantry awards. These medals were known as free ration medals and were awarded to all those who had served in some of these hard stations for a specific period of time.

During my short stay in Tezpur, I managed to get fairly good experience in the maintenance of Vampire and Toofani aircraft.

No. 101 Fighter Reconnaissance Squadron

Chapter 15

Air Force Technical College Bangalore

It was nice to be back in civilization again. It was only in 1960 that I had passed out of the portals of this institution and here I was back again.

I was given the subject of 'Propulsion' to teach the DEOs' Course and also given the job of Senior Technical Instructor (Engines) for the training of Technical Apprentices. The scheme for training apprentices to be inducted as technicians for the IAF, on the lines of AST, Hamble in UK had commenced in 1949, by selecting boys drawn from all over the country after a series of psycho-technical tests conducted at various centres in India. The boys were between fifteen to seventeen and half years of age, fresh after passing their matriculation examination. The streams were divided into seven important categories namely Airframes, Aero Engines, Aircraft Instruments, Electricals, Wireless, Radar and Armaments, and allotted according to the individual's aptitude. The training was for a period of four years after which they would pass out as Group 1 technicians.

The officers' courses running were the 18th and 19th DEO courses. As the 18th DEOs' course had almost completed their training, I started out by taking propulsion classes for the 19th DEO course. I went through the entire syllabus and found that most of the material had been covered in the course I had done for the AFRAeS exam. I dug up my lessons and prepared for the classes. The class was much larger than my course, 15 DEO and there were some very bright sparks in it.

There were three flight cadets in the course whom I had known earlier. One was Amat Sadanandan who was my classmate at Zamorins College in Calicut and had joined the Air Force as a Radar Operator before me. He had become a Senior NCO and had been selected for a commission in the Signals branch. The second was KHS Rao, whom I had mentored for the AMIE Exam in Electrical Engineering while we were both serving at Manauri and who was one of the three of us who had visited Benares in

1956. The third one was Bapat, an electrician ex-apprentice who was with me in No. 5 Squadron, who had also completed his AMIE course.

As Senior Technical Officer (STO) (Engines), my job was mainly supervisory. The instructional staff was all experienced Senior NCO's and Warrant Officers who had undergone the 'Methods of Instruction Course' and were trained instructors, unlike me with no instructional background. So, initially I would sit at the back of some classes to get to know the ropes of teaching fresh minds. After a month or so, when a new batch of apprentices arrived, I started taking the subject of preliminary engines. It was a pleasure to impart knowledge to these boys with no preconceived notion of things and had sharp minds eager to learn. Some of them later applied for commission as pilots and a few even rose to two-star rank.

I was staying in the officers' mess and there was another bachelor staying there who became a good friend of mine. His name was Flt Lt GS Panicker and he was the STI (Airframes). We started going out to town together by bus as neither of us had a vehicle. There were long waiting lists for the Lambretta and Vespa scooters. During one of my trips to Madras, my brother Bharathan who was with Ashok Leyland asked me whether I was interested in buying a Vespa scooter under their Manufacturer's Discretionary Quota (MDQ). I jumped at this and applied for a loan as soon as I got back. It was sanctioned quickly, my MDQ Vespa arrived and I was mobile and not bus-dependent anymore.

After No. 18 DEO passed out, a new course had arrived. This was No. 20 DEO and this course included two Naval Officers, Lt John David Panakkal and Lt Ananth, both engineers from the Aviation arm of the Indian Navy. This course was a large one and I was detailed to take the propulsion class for them as well. In the Officers mess, where both the trainees and staff dined, there was a separate table for the staff. The two Naval Officers were allowed to dine along with the staff. Soon, Panicker, Panakkal and me had teamed up, particularly for weekend outings and since Panakkal also owned a scooter, going to town was not a problem.

Gp Capt Narasimhan had taken over as the Commandant from Gp Capt MJ Kripalani. Wg. Cdr D Rajagopal was the Chief Instructor. They were keen on having cultural activities organized and Panicker was made in charge. He organized a couple of shows involving some latent talent among the trainees, both from among the officers and apprentice trainees, which were well received.

Some of the trainees from 19 DEO had enrolled in Snow's dancing school from where I had 'graduated' earlier. Snow had retired his earlier instructors and employed a couple of new ones who could tutor his trainees on new dances like the Samba and the Twist. After a few lessons, one of the officer trainees had complained to us that Snow was not what he seemed to be and that he was gay and had made a pass at him. Since he had made an official complaint, the matter was taken up and as a result, Snow's academy of dancing was placed 'Out of Bounds'. This puts an unsavoury end to the dance school, and they had to close it down as the trainee officers were the source of his income.

During the next vacation period, I decided to visit my folks in Madras by road on my scooter. I had to go solo as Panicker was going to Trivandrum and there was no one going to Madras.

I set out one morning and after going for about 3 hours, as I was approaching Vellore I started overtaking a slow moving bus. As luck would have it, there was a car coming at high speed from the opposite direction, and I swerved to avoid it and crashed into a mango tree. Apparently, I had flaked out. When I came to., a villager was trying to stem the flow of blood from the bridge of my nose and was using the juice of some leaves as an antiseptic.

Despite the accident, and as the scooter was not much damaged, I decided to push ahead. I reached home by evening and my brother Sathyan who was a house surgeon at the General Hospital, took care of the wound by giving me a couple of stiches and an injection and I was back in action again.

Sathyan had appeared for the ECFMG exam for proceeding to the USA, and had been declared passed and was awaiting the result of the matching programme, which would decide where he would be doing his medical internship in the USA. In February 1962, he left for New York where he started his internship at the Queens County Hospital, along with his classmate Rugmini, whom he later married in February 1963 in New York City.

When I got back, Panicker told me that Air Headquarters had asked for volunteers from officers of the Technical Engineering Branch for flight engineers' training and that he had already volunteered and that I should apply immediately if I was interested, as it was the last day for volunteering. I made out my application and handed it over to the adjutant.

One morning, the son of a cousin of mine from Calicut, Vinod, landed up at my room saying that he was interested in joining the Air Force as a pilot and he wanted to know what flying was all about. I told him that if he was interested in first-hand experience with flying I could help him. So on the next weekend, I took him to Jakkur aerodrome on the outskirts of Bangalore and gave him a ride on the flying club aircraft. They had just started a scheme of 'pay and get a joyride' for 15 minutes. He was hooked completely and the very next day went back and told his parents that he was joining the Air Force. Unfortunately, he had a problem with his eyes and could not clear his medicals. He later joined the Navy in the Executive Branch, retired as a Commander and then joined the Merchant Navy.

A month later, Panicker was selected to go to the Union of Soviet Socialist Republics (USSR) for training as a flight engineer on AN-12 aircraft. Sometime later, I was selected for training as a flight engineer on Mi-4 Helicopters. The AN-12 training was in a place called Lugovaya and the Mi-4 Helicopter training was in Frunze in Kirgizia. Neither of us had ever heard of either of these places.

Showing the Vice Chief around the engine section, AFTC, 1962

Chapter 16

Mi-4 Helicopter Training Frunze, Kyrgyzstan and Alma-Ata, Kazakhstan

Air Headquarters briefed us before our departure to Russia. Our group consisted of pilots, engineer officers, senior NCOs and airmen. The leader of the group was Sqn Ldr 'Spike' Gaekwad, a gregarious pilot who was slated to command one of the helicopter units later. The pilots were Johnny Dweltz, BS Bakshi, LK Datta, Kenny Dutton, Kaushik, Pereira, De Costa, Krishnan and a couple of others. The engineer officers were Pandit, Bhaskara Rao, Kidwai and myself.

We got our winter clothing organized and took off on March 1963, the first visit to a foreign country for all of us. Aeroflot was the only airline operating from India to the USSR in 1963. It was one of the oldest and largest airlines operating at that time. The aircraft which took us was the Ilyushin IL-18, a four-engined turboprop which was the mainstay of Aeroflot in the early 1960s. We had to land at Tashkent for a change of aircraft as the IL-18 was proceeding to Moscow. It was a great moment for all of us when we stepped out of the aircraft at Tashkent airport, the first foreign soil for all of us.

Tashkent ('Stone City' in Uzbek language) was the capital of Uzbek Soviet Socialist Republic (now Uzbekistan) and had been incorporated into the Russian Empire in the nineteenth century and into the Soviet Union in 1924. We spent a couple of hours at the airport restaurant where I tried the pilaf (a dish similar to biryani) and a dried fruit-based drink called 'Compote'. We were soon shepherded into a smaller aircraft and after an hour or so we landed at Frunze.

Frunze was the capital of Kirgizia (or Kirghiz SSR, now Kyrgyzstan), named after the renowned Russian Red Army Commander, General Mikhail Frunze after whom the Frunze Military Academy in Moscow is named.

The main street of the city was named Lenin Street and the other important street was named Sovietskaya Street, both of which were renamed after the dissolution of Soviet Union.

During the initial part of the training, the pilots, engineers and technicians were clubbed together for preliminary familiarization of the MI-4 helicopter (Mi-chithiree in Russian). The classes were conducted by a fat and fiftyish Lieutenant Colonel of the Soviet Air Force. The language of instruction was Russian, which none of us knew. So the interpreter would translate each sentence into broken English. Because of the mandatory time gap after delivery and absorption, the learning curve was not as steep as one would expect. After a couple of hours of lectures, we were granted a break known as a 'Papirosa' break. This meant a smoking break. Russian cigarettes were known as Papirosa, which were actually cylindrical-shaped cigarettes but only half filled with tobacco. One was supposed to pinch the empty part once, and then again after turning it over through 90 degrees before lighting up. Some of us who were non-smokers started smoking just for the sheer novelty of the experience.

The favourite alcoholic drink of the Russians was vodka, a spirit made with the express purpose of getting people sloshed. The lighter drink was 'piva' (local beer), the wholesome Russian patriotic beverage.

We were allowed to go out to town on weekends but were to be back by midnight. Some of the airmen used to visit the Frunze University campus and became friendly with the students. One of them, Corporal Daglish, a Jew from Cochin, was a good dancer and offered to give dancing lessons to the students They were quite enamoured of him as they were very keen to learn Western dancing.

During one weekend, some of us went to see an Indian movie, 'Love in Shimla' which was playing at Frunze Cinema, one of the two cinema halls in the city. We had to stand in line for more than 45 minutes to get the tickets. The film starred Joy Mukherjee and Sadhana in the lead roles. After the movie, we saw some Russian women in tears, paying a moist tribute to the sentimentality of the 'Indiski' movie. They were being consoled by some younger folks who were trying to tell these simple folks that 'It is only a movie, Babushka'.

After the ground training was over, the pilots started their flying training and the technical personnel were taken by bus to another city, Alma-Ata, for practical training on the maintenance of Mi-4 Helicopters which included an engine change and a main rotor change.

Alma-Ata ('Full of Apples' in the local language) was the capital of Kazakh SSR (now Kazakhstan). Later, the name was changed to Almaty and the capital was moved to Astana. The training at Alma-Ata was only for a month and we returned to Frunze by bus. Meanwhile, the pilots had completed their preliminary flying training. The technicians and technical officers were required to go back, except those who were being trained as flight engineers who had to stay back for flying training.

The flight engineers were known as 'Board Technics' and their training consisted of flying along with the pilots, standing on a ladder located in the cabin and monitoring the parameters of the engine and other systems of the helicopter. He was also required to look after maintenance requirements when the helicopter was outstation. We started our training along with our pilots. The problem was that we had to have an interpreter as well as the instructor, and there was only one ladder for all of us to stand on. The matter was somehow solved, as one of the instructor pilots knew a smattering of English and one of the interpreters was a qualified flight engineer as well.

Finally, all the pilots had done their solos; they had completed the designated flying hours along with flight engineers; and also passed the ground subjects, and thus the course came to an end.

We were taken by an Aeroflot flight to Tashkent and by an Aeroflot international flight back to Delhi. As soon as we reached Central Vista Mess in New Delhi we decided to go and have an Indian meal at Moti Mahal Restaurant in Old Delhi. That meal proved to be a gourmet meal for all of us, after eating kartofil (potatoes) and cutlets for more than ninety days.

We spent a few days in Delhi for debriefing at Air Headquarters and waiting for our posting orders. My posting was issued to 105 Helicopter Unit located at Jorhat in Assam.

I had to go back to AFTC to get my clearance and a week later, I boarded a train to Jorhat by the same route that I had taken in 1960 when I was posted from AFTC to No. 101 FR Squadron in Tezpur.

En route from Frunze to Alma-Ata, 1963

Chapter 17

105 Helicopter Unit Jorhat, Dinjan, Chabua

Jorhat was a much better place than Tezpur; at least I felt so, because the station had a reasonable mess, good rooms and being a large transport base, very good connectivity with the rest of the country.

The Station was commanded by Wg. Cdr Berry, known as 'Aunty Berry', and the Station was home to three units: No. 49 Squadron with Dakota aircraft under the command of Sqn Ldr 'Killer Mathews'; No. 104 Helicopter Unit with Alouette helicopters under the command of Sqn Ldr 'Satto' Williams; and No. 105 Helicopter Unit with Sqn Ldr KJ Mistry as the commanding officer. 105 Helicopter Unit had Bell G3 helicopters and was in the process of re-equipping with Mi-4 helicopters.

My commanding officer Mistry was an eccentric, grumpy, but lovable character, a Parsi from Bombay who had the unfortunate task of commanding a bunch of thugs, and almost all of them were Pilot Officers and a few Flying Officers, including me. All of us were bachelors and most of the pilots had undergone training in the UK: JD Bobb, MS Sekhon, Sreedharan, Harry Demos, Koshal, Sanger, 'Plokha' Vaid and 'Soorkhan' Suri are some names I can recall. Killer Mathews, OC 49, was a legendary Dak pilot who spent most of his time either in the cockpit or in the bar.

A supercharged Franklin engine powered the Bell 47G-3 helicopters of 105 HU. It was a pretty little machine with a full bubble canopy and skid landing gear. It could carry two passengers besides the pilot. It was also possible to carry two patients on special stretchers outside, above the skid landing gears.

The Franklin engine on two of the helicopters, however, had a peculiar problem. It was a thirsty engine – not for fuel but for oil. The engine oil would get exhausted before the fuel did. So the pilot had to carry a jerry can with engine oil when he went out on long sorties. When the oil warning light came on, he would, perforce, have to land, replenish the oil and carry on regardless.

Soon the full complement of Mi-4 helicopters and some more pilots arrived and we were asked to move to a place called Dinjan. Dinjan airfield, located about 12 km North-East of Chabua, is in the Dibrugarh district of Assam. It is located in the tea growing area and the closest town to it is Tinsukia. Dinjan airfield became prominent during Second World War when it became the launch airfield from where C-47 aircraft of the China National Aviation Corporation (CNAC) flew over the 'Hump' into Kunming in China carrying much needed supplies for the forces of Gen Chiang Kai-Shek for the war against Japan. Other similar airfields in the vicinity were Chabua, Ledo, Mohan Bari and Doom Dooma. The Dinjan airfield had been abandoned in 1945. The parent wing of Dinjan after its reactivation was No. 12 Wing, Chabua, and it was operating as a detachment of 12 Wing.

When we moved to Dinjan with our brand new Mi-4 choppers, we found the place overgrown with elephant grass, snakes, scorpions, very large mosquitos and different types of flying and non-flying insect species. The accommodation was, however, in regular though derelict buildings abandoned by the Brits or Americans or whatever, better than the 'bashas' of Tezpur. We got the area cleaned up and started operations, mostly to get the pilots fully operational on the Mi-4. We had to fly to Chabua often – a short 10-minute flight, as all administration facilities were located there, including the Accounts Section.

Wg Cdr John Dunbar Aquino, a tall lanky officer who looked like Sherlock Holmes without the pipe, commanded Chabua. A fighter squadron, No. 29 squadron, was also based at Chabua, commanded by Sqn Ldr Woodfall.

The only silver lining to life in Dinjan was a planters club nearby known as the Panitola Club where KJ used to take us on weekends in his jeep for wining and dining and general merrymaking.

We moved to Chabua and escaped the flora and fauna of the Dinjan area. We had to leave behind one of the Mi-4's, as it had gone on AOG due to want of spares. It soon became a Christmas tree as most of the parts from it had been cannibalized to make the other choppers serviceable.

An interesting aspect of life in Chabua was that after the Met briefing in the morning, all officers had to get back to the mess, where the Station

Commander, Wg. Cdr Aquino would address us on various topics, in his avuncular role. This was discontinued after he was posted out and Gp Capt Edul Jahangir Dhatigara took over.

Dhatigara was a bachelor and had won the Kirti Chakra during the Naga Operations. He was known for a culinary delight created by him known as Dhatigara Bhujia, which became a byword in Air Force messes. He was a frequent visitor to the bar where he used to order a tin of prawns, which would arrive spicily fried while he was on his second large whisky.

All our pilots had become fully ops on Mi-4 helicopters and were regularly called upon to mount sorties in support of the army, including casualty evacuation sorties. On one occasion, there was a message from the army that a soldier needed to be evacuated immediately as he had been seriously injured. A Mi-4 was launched with JD Bobb as pilot and MS Sekhon as co-pilot. They took off in the afternoon and landed at a makeshift helipad near the army unit. The injured soldier was carried inside together with a few soldiers proceeding on leave for whom a helicopter ride to civilization was a godsend. Bobb had readily agreed to take them on, despite the fact that the payload limit had been nearly reached.

He hurriedly took off as it was getting to be dusk and the before-sunset landing restrictions were strictly being imposed. He had to climb a bit to go above the clouds. A combination of high load, high speed and high altitude, apparently violated the aerodynamics of the rotor blades, which stalled. The helicopter started rolling and finally went down through some trees and crashed into the snow in the Mishmi hills, located at the junction of North-Eastern Himalayan and Indo-Burma ranges. Luckily, the leaves of the trees and the snow broke the fall and nobody was killed and none were seriously injured. They had to trek through the snow and find the nearest army post. Some of the soldiers had a rough idea where they were, and with the help of the injured soldier who was more knowledgeable than the rest of them, managed to take all of them to a remote army post. We got the message and a helicopter went and rescued them.

Although I was trained as a flight engineer, I was not eligible for a flying bounty, as the unit did not have an establishment for an officer flight engineer's post. So, I had applied for getting the establishment revised or to get me posted to a unit which did have such an establishment. While this decision was awaited, I decided to retrieve the helicopter on AOG, which we had left behind in Dinjan.

So, one morning we went to Dinjan along with a Queen Mary trailer and Pilot Officer Nari Narayanan, who had been posted as the Engineering Officer of the unit and a couple of airframe technicians. We found that a dog and her litter of four pups had made the fuselage their home. We removed the main rotor blades and lashed them onto the trailer and decided to take the helicopter without the rotor by road to Chabua. A tractor was quickly requisitioned and we set out in the wee hours of the morning to avoid traffic, with me in the Pilot's seat and Nari in the co-pilots' seat and an airman on top with a T-shaped wooden contraption. Now and then, the airman on top had to wield his T-shaped contraption to lift up electric wires which were overhead across the road to prevent their entanglement with the tail rotor pylon.

The ground sortie took 3 hours and we finally reached the main guardroom of Chabua base at 6 am in the morning. But we could not get in as the width of the helicopter was more than the width of the access way, even with gates fully open. Before this hiccup could turn into a hassle, we had to take a tactical decision before the station woke up. Nari and me took some pickaxes from the fire station nearby and broke the obstruction, ignoring the protests of the Sergeant on duty in the guardroom and taking full responsibility for the damage. We managed to get the tractor-helicopter into the camp and parked the chopper along with the others. I reported the matter to the security officer who had already complained to the commanding officer. I was then taken to the CO's office, expecting a dressing down. But Gp Capt Dhatigara excused me saying that, considering the larger picture, it was for a good cause.

A few weeks after the Mishmi hill crash, Eastern Air Command Headquarters told us that a team consisting of the principal of the Himalayan Mountaineering institute, Wg Cdr Singh, had been appointed to visit the accident site and salvage the helicopter. An officer of the Repair and Salvage Unit, Gauhati, Sqn Ldr Nanda and few airmen of his unit would also be part of the team. They required some volunteers from the unit to be part of the team as specialists to assist them. Corporal Barua, an airframe fitter, and I volunteered.

The salvage team consisting of six members, including me, was dropped at Hunli helipad located near a forward army camp. We stopped there for a day to make arrangements with the army folks to get some labourers organized, as they would be needed to carry back the salvaged parts. The next day we started out with great enthusiasm, which waned quite fast as most of us were not mountain climbers. On the second day, a wild boar attacked the party. The leader of the labourers had warned us to look out for animals in the area. He was well prepared with a bow and arrow. He killed the boar with one well-aimed arrow, which entailed a forced halt as the Mishmis had to make a meal of the wild boar using a makeshift barbeque.

Soon, we reached the snow line and progress became a bit tardy. To make matters worse, I tripped and fell and dislocated my ankle. One of the Mishmi chaps made a makeshift flint and helped me for the rest of the arduous climb. Finally, we reached the crash site of the helicopter, which was lying in an upside down position. We managed to salvage some critical components like instruments and radio equipment and started our descent back. The descent was harder than the climb as a different set of muscles had come into play. We totally got exhausted while reached the helipad. After staying overnight, we sent a message to base and soon a helicopter picked us up and took us back to Chabua.

After a month, there was a signal from Air Headquarters with commendations for all the participants of the salvage team – all except the two volunteers.

A month later, my promotion to Flight Lieutenant and posting to No. 110 Helicopter Unit, Tezpur, came through, to fill the flight engineer's post.

So, it looked like I was going back to my previous stomping grounds-to helicopters this time instead of fighters.

Chapter 18

No. 110 Helicopter Unit Tezpur and Helicopter Erection Unit, Santa Cruz, Bombay

I managed to get some leave before joining my new unit and so made a quick visit to Madras to see my folks.

The family had shifted to a new place in Santhome, close to Marina beach. My brother Bharathan was doing well in Ashok Leyland. His service manager, Mr Crook, an Englishman, and his immediate boss, Mr Browne had a lot of faith in his energy, ability and professional competence. They had appointed two more service engineers – Hyderabadwala, an experienced automobile engineer, and SK Nair who had passed out from Madras Institute of Technology, Chromepet.

My sister Sarala was enjoying her work at SIET Women's College, teaching chemistry. My younger brother, Sathyan had completed his MBBS and the mandatory House Surgeon's Training at the General Hospital. He was keen to go the USA for further studies and had cleared his ECFMG examination.

I cut my leave short as a 49 squadron Dakota was going back to Jorhat via Tezpur and I hitched a ride in that, thereby avoiding a 3-day journey by rail. Tezpur was a hive of activity with many choppers flying around. I got better accommodation this time as some old pucca buildings had been renovated and handed over to the Officers' Mess.

The Station was commanded by Gp Capt 'Pop' Bouche, a fighter pilot who had completed the entire eighteen-month course for Technical Engineering Officers at AFTC along with sixteen DEO, our junior course. He and 'Scorpy' Ghosh were the only pilots who had done this at that time.

Sqn Ldr 'Spike' Gaekwad was the OC of No. 110 Helicopter Unit. Flt Lt Rakesh Tandon was the Flight Commander. Among the pilots, Pratap Marathey and Kasturi were the senior guys. The other pilots were Neelu

Barve, De Costa, Pereira, Jacob Bell, Sreedharan, Kenny Dutton, Kaushik, Malik, LK Dutta (whose daughter, Lara Dutta, won the Miss Universe crown many years later) and some who had come through the Auxiliary Air Force route. Krishnan, Ram Mohan, Khosla, MN Singh, Goswamy and Mistry belonged to this group. Melville Rego, the Signals Officer from my senior course, was acting adjutant of the unit.

The unit was mainly tasked with logistics support for the army. We had to undertake sorties to places in Arunachal Pradesh like Ziro, Along, Walong, Daporijo, Tawangand and Pasighat, as well as sorties to helipads in Nagaland.

I started flying regularly as a flight engineer and had an opportunity to visit far-flung helipads. On one such flight, we had heavy vibration in the engine, which conked off suddenly. We had to auto-rotate and land on the banks of the Subansiri River in Arunachal Pradesh. We had messaged our base before landing. As we had spotted an army camp from the air, we set out searching for it and soon arrived at the camp. The guards on duty took us to the detachment commander who happened to be Major Rajagopal from the Potheri family of Cannanore. His brother was Air Cmde PC Ramachandran, AFC who used to be OC COM Squadron in Delhi. We had a drink together and the next day when our rescue helicopter arrived, we bid goodbye and came back to base. Before leaving, the Major requested me to hand over a jerry can of rum to his wife in Bangalore whenever I had a chance to hitch a Dakota ride to Bangalore. I managed to do so after a couple of weeks. The lady, who was from Goa, was delighted and offered me lunch.

Despite the fact that my primary job was that of a flight engineer, I had to mentor a young officer, Pilot Officer Jatti, who had been posted as the unit engineering officer, especially while supervising the tracking of the main rotor blades, which was a tricky operation. This was required to be carried out when the blades were out of track, resulting in vibration while flying.

We received a signal from Air Headquarters a few months after my arrival in Tezpur, detaching me to be officer-in-charge of the Helicopter Erection Unit at Santa Cruz, Bombay. It was a temporary job and I looked forward to my first independent assignment.

I arrived in Bombay as scheduled and reported to No. 2 Equipment Depot, located at Cotton Green. This was the only Air Force unit in Bombay and I was to give admin and logistic support to the Erection Unit. The rest was up to me and to two newly minted pilot officers of the Tech. Eng. Branch: Pilot Officer K Badrinarayanan and Pilot Officer PK Mukherjee. About twenty airmen and two senior NCO's were also posted to the unit.

We had to take an electric train from Cotton Green to Santa Cruz as we were not authorized any transport. We were told that there would be an audit objection if transport was provided to us. It was a problem commuting every day to and from Cotton Green to Santa Cruz and from there to the SWP hangar inside the airfield. We got around this problem by requisitioning a transport to convey the oxygen cylinders required for the servicing of the helicopters. As we did not have facilities at the hangar for storing oxygen cylinders with mandatory safety conditions, which were available only at Cotton Green, this was found permissible and we utilized this transport for commuting up and down.

After this admin problem solved, we started erecting the helicopters in full earnest. We were provided with four Russian specialists and a female Russian interpreter to assist us.

The erection ritual was as follows: the helicopters would arrive at the Sewri docks in a mother case and a number of smaller boxes in a ship from Russia. An inter-service unit called Embarkation Headquarters (which had an Air Force element under Sqn Ldr Parmanick) would get the cases unloaded from the ship and would inform me of their readiness to be transported. Since the load was very big, we had to requisition a Queen Mary trailer and get it moved from Sewri to Santa Cruz after midnight to avoid traffic hassles.

The cases were to be opened and inspected for transit damage in the presence of the Russians. The actual erection of the helicopters was a fairly simple procedure because the Russians were specialists in their field. Pilot Officer Badrinarayanan and Pilot Officer Mukherjee were of great help to me in getting the job completed in time. They also benefitted greatly in the process because, as a result of this grounding, they both became the kingpins in the Air Force on Mi-4 helicopters in particular and all subsequent Russian helicopters inducted into the Air Force in general, like the Mi-8 and Mi-17.

Once the erection was completed it had to be ground run, all systems were checked and if satisfied, I had to send a signal to Air Headquarters who would allot the aircraft to a particular unit. The unit would then send pilots to test fly and take over the helicopter and fly it out. The test flying would sometimes involve a number of sorties, which would depend on the pilots.

The Russians were missing their regular tots of vodka and occasionally I would find them missing. We later came to know that they had found a source of supply of country liquor in a village next to the airfield which they swore was almost as good as their Stolichnaya or Moskovskaya vodkas. When the villagers started fleecing them out of their limited supply of rupees and refused to accept rubles for payment, the Russians found a better solution for their alcoholic cravings. The Mi-4 helicopter has a system for de-icing the windscreen if it got iced up while flying. Spraying the windscreen with pure alcohol, which is stored in a small tank in the cockpit, clear the problem. The helicopter comes with this tank filled with the stuff and sealed. They used to break the seal and have a swig whenever they felt the urge. Since the windscreens in Indian conditions did not normally get iced up, this was seldom, if ever, used. So we ignored this, and unsurprisingly, their productivity increased remarkably thereafter.

On one occasion, when the cases which had arrived by Queen Mary trailer were opened, it was found that the trailing edges of twelve main rotor blades were damaged beyond repair. Each main rotor blade is about 10 meters in length and they were packed in very long pinewood boxes with four such blades in each box with their trailing edges facing up. There were three such boxes and the blades in all three had been found damaged. This would have delayed the erection of three helicopters until the arrival of the next ship from Russia. I called up Sqn Ldr Parmanick at Embarkation Headquarters and sent a signal to Air Headquarters. The Port authorities tried to pin the blame on the Air Force. They suggested that we must have damaged the blades while unloading them. A Court of Enquiry was held and the Russians and I had to appear before the court. We managed to sort out the diplomatic protocol involved in getting the foreigners to testify. Because of the testimony of the Russians, we were completely cleared of any neglect.

A few days later, I was informed that my promotion and posting had arrived and I was asked to hand over charge to Sqn Ldr Dalaya and report back to my unit at Tezpur. Accordingly, I got back to Tezpur by hitching a ride in one of the helicopters we had erected that had been allotted to 110 HU. My posting order stated that I had been posted to No. 6 Maritime Reconnaissance (MR) Squadron, Poona on promotion to the rank of Squadron Leader to fill the post of Flight Engineer Leader.

Before leaving for Bombay, I had made an application for a peace station posting as 'I wanted to get married before it was too late', and preferably to No. 6 Squadron, Poona to fill a flight engineer vacancy. It appears that the Director of Personnel, Gp Capt 'Ganja Bose', who was the CO of No. 11 wing Tezpur in 1960 when I was in 101 Squadron, told his deputy on seeing my application: 'This chap is still there? Post him wherever he wants!', or words to that effect.

My posting was the result. As one of my colleagues remarked, 'Jeeves is a lucky bastard!'

Chapter 19

No. 6 Maritime Reconnaissance Squadron Poona and Marriage

The squadron was originally formed in Trichinopoly on 1st December 1942 under the command of Sqn Ldr Mehar Singh. After a number of role transformations and types of aircraft, it was re-formed in January 1951 at Poona under the command of Sqn Ldr HK Goel with its new roles of MR and Air Sea Rescue, equipped with B-24 Liberators, which had been resurrected from salvage by a remarkable combination of HAL and the Air Force's collaborative effort. These were fitted with ASV-15A radar for its MR role.

In October 1961, nine Lockheed Super Constellation L-1049 aircraft, which had been retired from Air India, were added to the fleet, some of which were modified with ASV-21 radar for the MR role.

When I arrived at the squadron in March 1965, the squadron had a mixed fleet of Liberators and Super Constellations and was commanded by Wg Cdr VP Hegde, Vr. C, a decorated ex-Dakota pilot. There were a galaxy of experienced transport pilots, navigators, flight engineers, signallers and flight gunners on the squadron strength. Sqn Ldrs Ponnappa, Sadatulla, VBR Mishra, KD Kanagat, Bumpy Srivastava, Marwah and Flight Lieutenants AS Ray, BP Singh, Balsara Gopa Kumar, Vinod Kumar, Alagh and Sinha Ray were some of the pilots who were qualified on both types. The navigators included stalwarts like Dhagat, EPR Nair, Iyer and Shahul.

No. 2 Wing, the parent wing under which the squadron operated, was under the command of the youngest of the legendary Engineer brothers, Gp Capt Ronny Engineer, DFC. The other squadrons based at No. 2 Wing were No. 35 Squadron with Canberra bombers and No. 220 Squadron with Vampires.

I got accommodation in No. 1 Officers Mess where I shared a room with Flt Lt M Salahuddin who was officiating as Flight Engineer Leader of the squadron. He, besides being from my junior course, No. 16 DEO, had also studied at St Joseph's Boys High School, Calicut, but was a few years junior to me.

I took over as Flight Engineer Leader from Salahuddin, who introduced me to the flight engineers, which included some officers as well as a number of very senior Warrant officers and Senior NCOs. The officers included Rajadnya, Bhargava, Naresh Jain, Sadanandam, Ram Chandra and Ramakrishnan. All the officers were bachelors.

The posting to No. 6 Squadron was a prized posting for the aircrew, because the Super Constellations were operating a monthly courier flight to London and all Connie qualified aircrew would get a chance to go abroad once in six months or so. The squadron had to maintain a strict training protocol by which all aircrew had to qualify on Liberators before they could start training on the Super Constellations. This was inviolable regardless of who you were.

I too started my training on Liberators, which was comparatively easy for me as I had four years of experience in maintaining them.

I was on the wrong side of thirty years and wanted to settle down in life. As I was getting shunted between Tezpur, Jorhat, Dinjan and Chabua, I had not given serious thought to getting hitched. When I was on temporary attachment in Bombay for the helicopter erection work, my first cousin, MK Ramachandran of Burma Shell, had broached the subject and had even suggested a suitable match: a girl from Calicut from the well-known Kottieth family of Tellicherry who had just graduated. This had been conveyed to my folks back home and they had made some visits to Calicut and met the girl's parents and arranged a meeting between us. I made dash to Calicut for this ritual of seeing the girl. My cousin from Ganesh Nivas, Singer Damuettan's daughter Bharathy, enthusiastically organized a meeting. The venue for the meeting was near the Sreekanteswara temple. The girl, Bhagyam, had come, accompanied by two of her pretty nieces, Gita and Vidya. When I set eyes on her, I was struck dumb by her petite beauty and her large eyes and curly hair. She was pretty as a picture. We exchanged a few words and then she bid goodbye with a twinkle in her large eyes and slid away leaving a whiff of jasmine perfume in her wake. I am not sure if it was possible to see her without falling a little bit in love with her. It would be a massive understatement to say I was enraptured, hook, line and sinker. But would this beauty from the

Kottieth family of Tellicherry agree to tie the knot with a shortish, baldish, dusky fauji like me? That was the question.

Apparently she did. Things moved fast after the mutual agreement from both sides. The horoscopes had matched. There was an engagement ceremony and the date of the wedding was fixed for 27 June 1965. I was mentally getting prepared for peaceful married life in Poona.

Once the ice was broken, we started writing letters to each other. She had graduated in Zoology from Malabar Christian College with a First Class. She had four brothers and three sisters and had some fauji connections as well. Her elder sister was married to Lt Cdr Radhakrishnan of the Indian Navy, an uncle was a retired Major from the Indian Army, another uncle was the Scientific Advisor to the Chief of Army Staff and a cousin's husband was a Group Captain in the Air Force. One of her paternal uncles was a wing commander in the Air Force who later became the Accountant General of Orissa and was also posted to the Indian Embassy in Washington. He retired as the Auditor General of Southern Railways. So the pedigree was pretty good, better than mine.

The wedding finally approached and I was granted forty-five days annual leave. The wedding was to take place in Calicut where my future in-laws were living. As we did not have a house in Calicut, it was decided to have the wedding in Ganesh Nivas, where I had been staying during my student days. The venue, however, had to be changed as there had been a death in the Ganesh Nivas family and they were in mourning. So the venue was changed to Cannanore. Mr P Anandan, the husband of my first cousin Susheela, had agreed to host us and conduct the wedding in his house, Jayna. The bride's place where the ceremony would take place was at the Kottieth ancestral house in Cannanore.

It was raining a bit on the wedding day. The wedding party walked the short distance from the bridegroom's place at Jayna to the bride's residence at Kottieth house. It was a simple wedding with no elaborate rituals, followed by a simple meal.

After the wedding, we spent a few days in Cannanore, Tellicherry and Calicut before reaching home in Madras. My brother Bharathan arranged a second-hand Standard Herald two-door car, which I bought and decided to drive up to Poona via Bangalore. We had taken a driver named Ahmed along for the trip. My mother had also organized a cook, Ravi, for us to take with us to Poona.

And after spending one night in Bangalore with an old friend, Flt Lt Bhaskaran, we reached Poona after a couple of days. Before leaving Poona for the wedding, I had managed to get a house on rent organized in Poona town, as I had been wait-listed for service quarters and was allowed to rent a house on a rent-reimbursement basis. The house was in Nanapet, where Sardar Dastur, a Parsi gentleman, was staying. He was the head priest of the Parsi community. He had rented out a portion of his palatial house known as Dastur Hall to me and we headed straight for the place. Sardar Dastur and his wife had graciously arranged dinner for us at their place, which included a delicious dish called Bombay Duck.

We called on the Squadron Commander and the Station Commander as per Service protocol. The squadron had also arranged a party for welcoming the newly married couple. The party included ballroom dancing and my wife took to it as if long accustomed to it although she had never danced before.

My training as a flight engineer on Liberators finished well before the scheduled date for completion and I started flying on MR (Maritime Reconnaissance) sorties. They were very long sorties over the Arabian Sea.

We had one visitor during our stay in Dastoor Hall. My brother Bharathan visited us during an official trip to Poona. He recalled that my wife had mentioned to him about one of her distant cousins who was working in Maharani Gayatri Devi School in Jaipur who he thought would be a real good match for him. He gathered some more information about her. He did not pursue the matter any further with us and left after a couple of days. We came to know later that he had made a quick dash to Jaipur and visited the school and proposed to her.

After the necessary family consultations, they decided to get married.

We left Dastoor Hall when a house was allotted to me at No. 4 Naylor Road in Koregaon Park. It was a large duplex house – the upper floor was allotted to me and the lower floor to Sqn Ldr Marwah, a pilot of our squadron. The large bungalow behind us was where the Station Commander, Gp Capt Ronny Engineer, was staying. We had a great time here as it was right in the middle of the Civil Lines area and close to Main Street and East Street, where the good restaurants and movie houses like the West End and New Empire cinema halls were located. The drive to work in Lohegaon, where the Air Force Station was located, was a long one, but Marwah and I started sharing cars on alternate days.

My turn for the Super Constellation training came up soon. There were quite a few top class instructors such as Warrant Officers Shankar, Swami, Martin, Lakshmanan, KR Menon, KPK Menon and others.

Meanwhile, Salahuddin's wedding was also coming up. A Super Constellation cross-country training flight was arranged to coincide with Salahuddin's wedding to Goushya at his residence in Cathedral Gardens in the city, where I met his elder brother Naimuddin who had studied with me in Calicut from 1945 to 1949. The bride and bridegroom moved into Dastoor Hall, which I had vacated earlier.

I finally completed my training and started flying in Super Constellations as a qualified flight engineer. As Air India was carrying out periodic inspections of the aircraft as they had the infrastructure to do it, we had to make frequent short trips to Bombay, which gave me ample opportunity to consolidate my practical experience. The Super Constellation aircraft was so designed and configured that the flight engineer had a hands-on role in its operation, unlike the Mi-4 helicopter where the role was limited to an observational and a monitoring one, and the Liberator where it was slightly more, but still limited to non-critical areas of operation.

Once I got my categorization by the Categorization Board, I was eligible to be rostered for courier service to UK. My first trip to the UK was scheduled for June 1966.

My wife Bhagyam, 1965

AT OUR WEDDING ON 27 JUNE 1865

Kottieth House, Tellicherry

Chapter 20

No. 6 Squadron Pune-UK Couriers

My wife had become pregnant with our first child. When she was about three months into her pregnancy, she had some obstetric problems for which we had to consult a lady doctor on Main Street, Poona. She was a family doctor named Davierwala who suggested complete bed rest and also prescribed a drug named Duphaston. Although our cook Ravi was there to help, we needed a lady in the house. I requested my mother and she readily agreed and arrived in Poona escorted by my sister Sarala. They stayed for a couple of months till my wife had recovered.

My first flight as crew of the UK courier took place in June 1966. We had a briefing at Air Headquarters and left for our first leg to Jamnagar where we stayed overnight. The next morning we took off for Bahrain, which took about 7 hours. The captain of the aircraft was Sqn Ldr KD Kanagat who used to be the detachment commander at Srinagar in 1958 while I was there a part of the No. 12 Squadron detachment.

We stayed overnight at the Royal Air Force base at RAF Muharaq airport. It was a 24-hour halt, but we had time to go shopping at Navy Army Air Force Institute (NAAFI) shopping centre, from where I bought a Sony Tape Recorder and a Moulinex mixie for my wife from the meagre foreign exchange given to us. The following day we took off for Beirut after taking on a full load of fuel.

Beirut, the capital of Lebanon, was considered the Paris of the Middle East with most of the hotels marketing themselves as 'Every room facing the Mediterranean'. The city still retained the French influence as Lebanon was under the French Mandate after the collapse of the Ottoman Empire. They had got their independence in 1943. It was a banking haven and a great tourist centre for the rich and famous until the Lebanese civil war broke out in 1975, lasting for fifteen years.

We had a 2-day halt in Beirut, which we utilized to the fullest extent. The cuisine was delicious with items like kibbeh – a dish made of cracked wheat, minced onions and finely ground lean beef, lamb, and goat or camel meat. Shawarma was a meat preparation where lamb, chicken, veal or mixed meats were placed on a spit (commonly a vertical spit in restaurants), and might be grilled for as long as a day. Shavings were cut off the block of meat for serving, and the remainder of the block of meat was kept heated on the rotating spit.

After two days of culinary enjoyment, we took off for Orly Airport, Paris for a day's stay. As it was the first visit to Paris for some of the crew, we did the Eiffel Tower during the day and the Moulin Rouge at night and were captivated by the can-can dancers and the cabaret shows. By this time, our foreign exchange was getting rapidly depleted, so we called it a day for the time being.

The next day we took off for London's Northolt airport, which was the Royal Air Force Base located North of Heathrow airport in the South Ruislip area. During the Battle of Britain, this airport was the home of the Royal Air Force and the Polish Air Force fighter squadrons.

In London, we would be staying for a week. We were booked in a hotel in the Strand known as the Stand Palace Hotel, located in the theatre district of London near Covent Garden. We reported to the Air Attaché's office at South Audley Street as per protocol and spent the rest of the day sightseeing. I visited Madam Tussaud's Wax Museum where Mahatma Gandhi, Alfred Hitchcock and some others were displayed. In the Chamber of Horrors, one could see Adolf Hitler, Jack the Ripper and sundry other notorious murderers of history.

As we were rapidly running out of foreign exchange, we started having a sumptuous late breakfast in the hotel, which was part of the tariff, and either skipped lunch or had a sandwich from the food courts of department stores in Oxford Street.

On the penultimate day in London, I did some shopping from Mothercare for my wife and got some gifts for friends. On our return, we came back via Le Bourget airport in Paris, Beirut and Jamnagar.

After my return, we started getting visitors at our Naylor Road residence. My wife's cousin, Prabha, had landed up one day to look around Poona and to visit her alma mater, the famous Wadia College of Poona. Later, my first cousin Madhavan and family came and stayed with us on their return from East Africa, where he had worked for many years.

We moved to the ground floor of the house as Marwah had been allotted service accommodation inside the Air Force station. We had more house guests – Sreedharan (from Moody's Tea Estate) and his wife Sati with their children Satish and Sandesh on their way to a North Indian motoring holiday, shortly followed by KV Radhakrishnan, of Burmah Shell, Bombay with his wife Raji and children Brinda and Ammu. My wife's sister Sita and her husband Lt Cdr Radhakrishnan with their son Manu also stayed with us for a while on their transfer from Cochin to Bombay, pending their house allotment at Dhanaraj Mahal in Bombay.

I moved to regular service accommodation in October 1966 at 322A New Project. I got the lower floor of the house while the upper floor was allotted to Flt Lt Lal Sadarangani, who was a fighter pilot in 220 Squadron (he was later a POW in Pakistan).

After moving to the house, I took some short leave to take Bhagyam to her home in Calicut for her confinement. The due date was estimated as the first half of December 1966.

Since I was alone for the next few months, I piled up some more hours of flying, mainly on the Assam Courier to Gauhati via Delhi and Bagdogra, and occasionally for trips to Car Nicobar. There were lots of volunteers for the CarNic trips, ostensibly for collecting coconuts from there by the sackful, but mainly for the collateral benefit of goggling at the topless female tribals of the island.

My next UK courier trip came up in December 66. The crew was different from the previous one. We did the direct route from Jamnagar to Beirut and skipped the stopover at Bahrain. In Beirut, some of us explored the Jeita grotto located about 18 km away, where we were taken by boat into the grotto which has an upper cave and a lower cave. The upper cave contains a great concentration of a variety of crystallized stalactite and stalagmite formations which were breath-taking. The leg from Beirut to Northolt via Paris was routine.

On our return leg, we had two days at Paris. I visited the Louvre on Sunday when the admission was free and spent the whole day there. I was particularly fascinated by the self-portrait of Leonardo da Vinci displayed in one of the halls. The portrait is drawn in red chalk on paper. It depicts the head of an elderly man in three-quarter profile view, turned towards the viewer's right. The subject is distinguished by his long hair and long waving beard, which flowed over the shoulders and chest. I bought a print of this, which I later got framed and it still hangs in my house. In the evening, we visited the Crazy Horse Saloon to see the spectacular cabaret show. The dancers were outstandingly sensual and cheeky and the performances were precisely and elegantly choreographed. During the interval, there was a magic show by an Indian, who was a Mallu immigrant from Mahe who had taken French citizenship.

We landed back in India on schedule and immediately proceeded on leave as my wife was expecting the baby any time. I arrived at Calicut on 12 December and as the train was slowing down at the platform, my wife's younger brother Ravi spotted me and came running along the slowing train, shouting 'It is a boy! It is a boy!' to the amusement of my fellow passengers. It seems the baby was born that very day at 10:30 am at the Government Beach Hospital. We named the boy Vasant on the 28th day, all decked up in the clothes I had got from Mothercare in Oxford Street in London. We returned to Poona in February via Madras to show him off to my folks.

We had a new Squadron Commander, Wg. Cdr JB Lal, who had earlier been in P staff at Air Headquarters, a very fine gentleman who was a father figure to all of us. The Station Commander had also changed since Ronny Engineer had put in his papers in a huff as he had been rather unfairly blamed by a Court of Enquiry for a Canberra aircraft accident, which had been damaged during a night landing because it had hit a cow which had strayed onto the runway. He was blamed as he was the commanding officer of the station where it had occurred.

His replacement was Gp Capt Surinder Singh, who had a fetish for physical fitness and made it a rule that no officer of the station would be granted annual leave unless he could run a mile in 8 minutes. Although it was double Roger Bannister's timing, very few of us could make the grade. One could often see people panting during practice runs with a sports officer timing them with a stopwatch.

During the Annual Confidential Reports, known as P-57s, the commanding officer of the squadron would interview us individually for a confidential chat. JB Lal told me something during my interview that simultaneously pleased me and troubled me. He told me that P Staff had empanelled me for a postgraduate course at the Cranfield Institute of Technology, UK. But they had then dropped my name as the Technical Directorate had advised them that Cranfield would not accept me as I did not have a university degree and my qualification of being a graduate of the Royal Aeronautical Society, London, would not be acceptable. My CO also told me that he was informing me about this as he had received a call from the Director of Engineering at Air Headquarters who had given this advice to the P Staff. He had called to find out the name of the flight engineer who was proceeding for the next UK courier. My CO told me that I could expect call from him in a couple of days.

In fact, I got a call from him the same day. He asked me to get him a refrigerator from England, which would be handed over by someone from the air attaché's office in London. I told him it would not be possible as we had standing instructions not to violate any customs regulations. After the call, I informed my CO about the call and he told me that I had done the right thing in refusing the request.

I wrote to the Cranfield Institute and requested them to let me know if my qualification barred me from admission to their postgraduate course. They wrote back to say that it was very much acceptable and that in fact an officer of the Indian Navy who had the same qualification was undergoing the course right then. I did not pursue the matter further, as I would have been over age for the next course in any case.

Chapter 21

A VIP Flight

The Aircrew Examining Board was arriving at No. 6 Squadron to categorize the aircrew. During their last visit, I had been categorized as Cat B. On this visit, I was examined both in theory and flying for upgradation to Cat A which would enable me to be part of the crew to fly VVIP passengers. After the test, I was upgraded to Cat A.

We got information that the Chief of Air Staff, Air Chief Marshal Arjan Singh, would be visiting the UK at the invitation of the Chief of the Royal Air Force to review the passing-out Parade of the RAF Cadets at Cranwell. This was a great honour to him in particular and to the IAF in general as he was an alumnus of RAF Cranwell and had passed out from there in December 1939.

The Chief decided to travel to UK in our courier aircraft instead of travelling by Air India. Mrs Arjan Singh, his staff officer Wg Cdr Kapoor and his ADC Sqn Ldr Jaiswal would accompany him.

An all officer aircrew was selected for this flight. Sqn Ldr Ponappa, Sqn Ldr Sadatulla and Flt Lt SM Mehra were the pilots, who were all qualified captains. Flt Lt Shahul and Fg Offr Mitra were the navigators. Fg Offr Rajadnya and I were the flight engineers and Sqn Ldr Gulzar Singh was the Air Signaller.

After a special briefing by Air Headquarters, we took off for Jamnagar with our chief, his wife and staff. The flight plan was Delhi–Jamnagar–Cairo–Rome–Paris–London (Northolt). The chief would be visiting the IAF training team in Cairo en route. The team had been posted there to train Egyptian Air Force pilots.

We were received at Cairo airport by the chief of the Egyptian Air Force and W Wg. Cdr CKS Raje, the leader of the IAF Training team and a celebrated transport pilot. We were accommodated in a hotel in the city. As we would have a 2-day halt in Cairo, Raje had arranged a quick sightseeing tour for us; we saw the pyramids and went for a cruise on the Nile.

After the 2-day halt, we went to Rome for a day's halt and then on to Northholt. The flight from Rome to Northolt was a short one, but the crew were told that we should arrive on the dot as the chief of the Royal Air Force would be present to receive our chief at Northolt with a full ceremonial Guard of Honour, and the door should be opened at exactly at 09:00 hours. We landed at 08:50 and started our taxiing and exactly at 08:59 hours, we arrived at the designated spot. Meanwhile, the chief was ready in his ceremonial uniform, standing at the door ready to step out. The signaller turned the big door handle counter clockwise to open the door but the door got stuck. He tried again and again but the thing would not budge. The chief quietly nudged him aside and with a flick of his hand turned the handle. The door opened and he straightened himself to his full six feet and stepped outside as the RAF band struck up the national anthem.

The chief would be busy for next few days with ceremonial functions as the guest of the Royal Air Force, so we carried on with our normal routine.

We would be returning without the chief and Mrs Arjan Singh as they had an extended programme. But his staff officer and the ADC would be returning with us in the courier aircraft. We took the normal route via Paris and proceeded to Beirut. The day after we landed at Beirut, the Arab–Israeli War, also known as the Six-Day War, broke out. The date was 5 June 1967.

There had been growing tension between Egypt and Israel for a while. On 5 June, Israel launched a spectacular series of pre-emptive airstrikes against Egyptian airfields. The Egyptians, whose defensive infrastructure was in a poor state, were caught completely by surprise and virtually the entire Egyptian Air Force was destroyed with very few Israeli losses, giving the Israelis complete air superiority. Simultaneously, the Israelis launched a ground offensive into the Gaza strip and through the Northern and central routes of the Sinai, which again caught the Egyptians by surprise. After some initial resistance, the Egyptian leader, Gamal Abdel Nasser, ordered the evacuation of the Sinai. On June 6 and 7, Israeli forces rushed Westward in pursuit of the Egyptians whose retreat was disorganized and chaotic.

Our further progress would not be possible as the air space on our route would be unsafe. We were summoned by the Indian Ambassador Mr Appa Pant who instructed us after consulting Air Headquarters to fly out of Beirut and proceed to Larnaca in Cyprus and say put there until further notice.

We landed in Larnaca and got accommodation in Ledra Palace Hotel in Nicosia. As the duration of our stay was indefinite, we started sightseeing, as we would probably never see this country again. The people were mostly of Greek origin and the rest were of Turkish origin. There was tension between the two: there was a Greek sector and a Turkish sector in the capital city of Nicosia.

The hotel started filling up with war correspondents, mostly from Western countries. Some of them became friendly with us when they learnt we had just arrived from Beirut. One of the correspondents was Winston S Churchill, the grandson of Sir Winston Churchill. He had subsequently written the 'The Six-Day War' along with his father Randolph Churchill, a book that gives a graphic account of the Arab–Israel war.

One of the British war correspondents told us about a fabulous show in the Turkish section of the town where he said the best belly dancing in the world could be seen. We got the necessary permits organized and set out next evening to see the show. As only one seat was available in the front row, it was agreed that the senior most person of our group could take that seat and the rest of us would take the back seats. So Wg. Cdr Kapur, the staff officer of the chief was given the honour. The show was very engrossing – indeed so engrossing that at the end of the show, Kapur realized that his wallet had been pickpocketed while he was watching the gyrations of the sultry Turkish sirens on the stage. We got back to the hotel and held a council of war where we decided to pool in our remaining foreign exchange and contributed a kitty for Kapur, so the poor man did not have to starve for the rest of our stay.

After a week, when the war ended, we were given clearance to leave. We set course for a direct flight to Jamnagar and then on to Delhi for debriefing and for dropping off our two passengers.

The squadron anniversaries were fabulous affairs – mostly theme parties like a shipwreck party, Arabian Night party, village theme party and for all of which the mess was decked out spectacularly to reflect the theme. For the village theme party, VBR Mishra arrived in a real bullock cart with his wife demurely sitting inside it. For the Arabian Night party, some hired costumes from drama companies in Poona city and for the Christmas party, a Christmas tree was flown in from Srinagar in the cargo version SuperConnie. The guests were served rum punch from an astrodome salvaged from an old Liberator.

For one such anniversary, the invitation was like a summons, which said at the end "Thou shalt ignore these summons at thy peril'

The RSVP from the Navy was as follows:-

FROM INS DELHI FOR SUMMONS FROM 6 SQUADON
"EYE" IN COMMAND AND ALL MY OFFICERS ON BOARD
WOULD GLADLY ANSWER YOUR SUMMONS IN HORDE
TO DINE AND DRINK AND DANCE WITH THE DRAGON
FOR NONE OF US ARE REALLY ON THE WAGON.

ALAS IT IS OUR TASK AT TIMES TO PUT OUT TO SEA
AND LIVE A LIFE NOT SOLELY EASE AND LUXURY
WHEN COMFORTS AND THIS WARMTH FOR CELEBRATION
BECOME A RATHER VAGUE AND DISTANT CONTEMPLATION
THUS 'EYE' AND ALL MY THUGS, UNWORTHILY DECLINE
YOUR KIND AND AND GRACIOUS SUMMONS TO THIS WINE

AND LEAVE THE JOYS OF ALL THE MINI SKIRTED LASSES
TO THE TEUNDER MERCIES OF OTHER HUNGRY MASSES
AND SOME ADVICE BEFORE I END THIS NOTE
(I HAVE LEARNT FROM MUCH EXPERIENCE ON THIS BOAT)
BE NOT MISLED BY SKIRTS BELOW THE KNEE
THEY PICK IT UP AND RUN WITH EQUAL EASE

MASTER INS DELHI

The upgradation of the station commander to the rank of Air Commodore resulted in the posting out of the incumbent physical fitness freak, Groupy Surinder Singh. Air Commodore Idris Latif was posted as our new Air Officer Commanding (AOC) the station. He had just completed a distinguished stint as the Air Attaché in the Indian Embassy in Washington. The AOC and his wife, Mrs Idris Latif, were a charming, cultured, sophisticated couple.

The AOC started a routine of periodic lectures to be delivered by officers of each squadron in turn on selected subjects. The lectures would be delivered on Saturdays in the station cinema hall and all officers were expected to attend.

As I had put in my name to appear for the Defence Services Staff College Entrance examination in 1968, my CO had asked me to select a suitable subject to be delivered by me when our squadron's turn came up.

I selected the subject 'India and the Bomb', and delivered the lecture as scheduled. As the subject was controversial, there were lots of questions at the end of the talk. Anyway, it was a very good experience to address a large knowledgeable group.

My folks in Madras had shifted to another rented house near Mowbrays Road in Madras. My brother had finally got married to Ambujem of Gayatri Devi School. She was known as one of the 'Jem' sisters as all the girls in her family had names ending in the word 'Jem' – Ambujem, Pankajem, Sarojem, Shylajem, Jalajem and Padmajem. There were no more girls as they probably ran out of any more Jem names and switched to boys – three of them bringing the tally to a grand total of nine children.

The wedding was in Bangalore, which we attended. My brother had got a spacious house, provided by the company, on Greenways road in Adyar after his promotion as the Assistant Service Manager at Ashok Leyland.

My younger brother, Sathyan had moved to Toronto in June 1967 and he stayed on there for a year and acquired the FRCP from Toronto University.

I appeared for the Staff College exam along with a few others and was very lucky as usual, because there were questions on the use of air power during the Arab–Israeli war of 1967, which I had pretty good knowledge of as I had been around that area when it happened.

The results came out the following month. I had passed and would have to proceed to Wellington in the Nilgiris in January 1969.

Before the course commenced, all the passed candidates had to attend a four-week course at the Institute of Armament Technology at Girinagar, Poona. As it was located quite a distance from Lohegaon, we had to commute every day to and from the Institute. As I had a car, some of the candidates from outstation would hitch a ride with me. Wg Cdr 'Chotu' Bhakle and Sqn

Ldr PM Ramachandran, two of the fighter pilots who had qualified, were my daily commute companions.

We received detailed joining instructions from the Staff College to enable them to allot accommodation, arrange admission for children in the Staff College School and to allocate maidservants.

We received our posting orders, and after the usual send-off parties, prepared to leave Poona to a completely different environment.

Chapter 22
Defence Services Staff College Wellington

The Staff College course was scheduled to start in January 1969 and would last a year. We took the train from Poona to Madras and stayed for a few days with my folks there. From Madras, we boarded the Mettupalayam Express and from there we had the delightful experience of travelling by the Nilgiri Mountain railway train. These are meter gauge trains with open wooden compartments and pulled using a rack and pinion system by what are known as X-Class coal-fired locomotives. On some sections, the gradient was as steep as 1:12.5. These locos were imported from Switzerland in the 1920s and it was a delight travelling on this route. Many of the Air Force and Army types proceeding to the Staff College in Wellington were on the train, headed for Coonoor.

We arrived at Coonoor station where a reception group was waiting for us, which included a JCO and a couple of soldiers who helped us to a transport which took us to the house allotted to us called Pleasant View, near the Upper Coonoor post office. A maid was waiting for us at the house. It was a small house with two bedrooms, a drawing room and a dining room and kitchen. The Staff College had a formula for allotment of houses. The type of house would depend upon factors like seniority, rank, number of children and the kind of vehicle you owned. Those without vehicles would be given rooms in Wellington Hall, close to the College. There were a number of foreign students from countries like the USA, UK, Malaysia, Nigeria, Iraq, Afghanistan, South Yemen, Zambia and Canada who were also given accommodation in Wellington Hall. The overflow from there would get it in a place called Circle Quarters.

The DSSC Wellington was formed in 1948 after DSSC Quetta (in present-day Pakistan) was closed down in 1947, following the division of the country. The purpose of the college in the words of an ex-commandant of the college, Lt Gen Billimoria, was 'It is here at Staff College, the think tank of the Services, that the middle rank officers of the Indian Armed Forces and selected civil servants upgrade their knowledge from the mechanics of soldiering to the level of conception of ideas in the sphere of military, socio-political, economic and scientific fields, and integrate them into the larger aspects of national life'.

Our course was the No. 25th Staff Course and we were twenty-two officers from the IAF, one from the IAS and one from the Ordnance Department. The IAF element had pilots, navigators, engineering branch officers and an education branch officer, all of Squadron Leader rank except one, Wg. Cdr Bhakle. There were ten fighter pilots, including Sqn Ldr Lavender from the RAF, two bomber pilots, two transport pilots and one helicopter pilot. There were three navigators, one signals officer, two engineer officers and one officer from the education branch.

The Directing Staff (DS) was headed by the Chief Instructor (Air), Gp Capt VM Bhatnagar. The other DS were Wg Cdr PP Singh MVC, Wg. Cdr PS George, Wg Cdr OM Kunhiraman, Wg Cdr ML Sethi and Wg Cdr MB Krishnamurthy, who was the DS (Coord) and looked after admin matters as well.

Each student officer was allotted a locker with a number, where all letters, instructions and assignments would be deposited. Once done, the completed assignments would have to be deposited in the locker of the DS concerned, strictly by the specified time and without exceptions.

We were given individual exercises and syndicate exercises. In addition, each student had to deliver one small speech on a selected subject and one long speech. Some syndicates would be with the army wing and some would be combined with all three wings.

One of the short speeches I had to deliver was on Flight Refuelling and the long one was on Communism. I selected this topic for the long speech because I had first-hand experience of the practical aspects of communism during my training in USSR in 1963.

One of the colourful characters of the course was 'Mackie Palamkote', a bomber pilot whose conversation was rich in bilingual four-letter swear words in an intriguing combination of English and Punjabi. While the subjects chosen for the long lecture by most of us were on subjects like Strategy, Air Power, Nuclear Second Strike capability and similar heavy stuff, he chose the subject 'Fishing' as the topic of his hour-long talk, illustrated by the picture of a long rainbow trout on the blackboard.

During one combined exercise when the entire college was present, and while my course mate Bindra and me were engaged in some frivolous conversation during a dull lecture by an army DS, we were caught off guard, as we could not answer question put to us, since we were not listening. It was a humiliating moment for both of us and for the Air Wing. After the exercise, we were hauled up before the CI and given a massive dressing down. On a subsequent day, during a similar exercise being conducted by an Air Force DS on a subject connected with nuclear first strike and second strike, he posed a tricky question, which no one could answer. As usual, Dame Luck favoured me as I had done some deep study of the subject when I had to deliver the lecture on 'India and the Bomb' while at Poona. So I got up and answered the question, which pleased the CI no end and my earlier transgression was forgiven and soon forgotten.

We had an industrial all-India tour scheduled soon, for which an entire train would be requisitioned. We boarded the train at Mettupalayam and proceeded to Madras and then on to Bombay. The officer-in-charge of the train was a fine Army officer, Lt Col Nanda from Coorg, who later rose to become the Vice Chief of Army Staff. The train had all the facilities you would need, including even a barber with his entire paraphernalia. After visiting some industrial establishments, we embarked on a cruise in the Indian Navy tanker 'INS Deepak', which took us from Bombay to Cochin where we visited the Naval Signals Training establishment.

The social life in the college was vibrant, as in any Army run establishment. The College Amateur Dramatics Society (CADS) staged regular plays, including one which parodied the training programme in an exceedingly whimsical way.

They also had a show depicting the brides of India from all the States of the country. Bhagyam was selected to represent the bride from Kerala.

We had some officers on the course who had already won gallantry awards during the 1965 war. In fact, one of our DS, Wg Cdr PP Singh had won the Maha Vir Chakra during the 1965 war while commanding a Canberra squadron, and one of the student officers, Sqn Ldr Kahai had been awarded the Vir Chakra during the same war. Sqn Ldr PM Ramchandran had been decorated with the Shaurya Chakra during the Goa operation in 1961. He later completed the test pilots' course at the Empire Test Pilots' School at Boscombe Down, UK and later was appointed as the AOC-in C of an Operational Command in the rank of an Air Marshal. Sqn Ldr Pratap Rao would also get a three-star rank and become the Vice Chief of the Air Force.

The star student officers from the Army wing were Major Bipin Joshi and Major Shankar Roy Chowdhry who would both rise to become Chiefs of the Army Staff. Major Chibber was appointed Governor of a State after he retired as a Lt General and Major Khanduri joined the BJP party after retiring as a Major General and became the Chief Minister of Uttarakhand.

Meanwhile, my brother Sathyan had come back to India under the Government of India's technology transfer programme. He had passed the FRCP exam from Canada. I had met him in London during a UK courier trip in September 1968, while he was on his way back to India along with his wife Dr Rugmini and their two-year-old daughter, Shalini. They had set up a Pediatric Hematology laboratory at the Children's Hospital in Madras and after a year of working in Madras, had decided to go back to New York. In October 1969, they were on their way to Ottappalam in Kerala to see Rugmini's folks. We drove down with our young son Vasant to Coimbatore to meet them.

Throughout our stay in Coonoor, we would make frequent trips to Gudalur on the other side of Ooty to visit my wife's sister for weekends of relaxation in their tea estate, called Heath Field Estate.

On other weekends, we would go to play cards with some of our relatives living around the Coonoor area. So life in Wellington was not all work and no play.

The course came to an end in December 1969 and we all waited for our posting orders. The CI announced it one morning. I was posted as Assistant Director in the TS 1 section of the engineering branch of the Air Force directly under the Director of Engineering, the same Air Officer who had asked me to get a refrigerator from UK and which I had declined to do. I knew my goose was cooked!

25th Staff Course, Staff College (Air Wing), 1969

Sathyan, Rugmini and Shalini, New York 1969

Chapter 23

Air Headquarters New Delhi

I reported to Air Headquarters at RK Puram in New Delhi where the Maintenance Branch, headed by the Air Officer-in-Charge Maintenance (AOM) was located. The incumbent AOM was Air Marshal YV Malse, an officer of the Flying Branch.

The Director of Technical Services, under whom I had been posted as ADTS-1, controlled all technical services. He had under him a number of Deputy Directorates – TS1, TS2, TS3 and so on. TS1 was more of a Technical Administrative Directorate dealing with the issue of technical staff instructions, policy letters, etc. The Director was an Air Commodore (later upgraded to Air Vice Marshal). I was posted as ADTS-1. My immediate superior was DDTS-1.

On arrival, I was taken by my DD to meet the Director who had engineered my posting under him. He was close to superannuation and my first interaction with him was a formal and a grim affair.

As I did not get service accommodation, I took up a house on reimbursement basis in a colony known as Shanti Niketan, an upstairs two-bedroom flat, with the landlord staying downstairs. My immediate neighbour was Sqn Ldr VGI Subramanian, a Logistics branch officer who had just arrived after a posting to the UK as Assistant Air Attaché. His wife, Prema, soon took up a teaching job in a neighbouring school named Little World Nursery School, where we put our three-year-old son, Vasant.

I did not expect smooth sailing under my director, but again Lady Luck smiled on me. Three months after my arrival, I got a call from the staff officer to the AOM that I was wanted by the AOM. I was only a junior squadron leader and not dealing with any serious issues, so I was intrigued by this call. I informed my boss about the summons and quickly presented myself before the big man. He interviewed me for 15 minutes, asked me about my professional experience and personal background and after this, he fixed me with his glittering eye and told me that from the next day onwards I would be working as his technical staff officer. I was not particularly keen to work as a staff officer, which I thought was like a glorified personal secretary, but I had no choice and the silver lining on the cloud was that I would be getting out of the clutches of my director and this was an exit strategy worth my while. Besides, the AOM already had a smart young staff officer, Flt Lt Jaitley to look after his personal affairs and my job would be purely professional. Later, Jaitley confided in me that the AOM had been looking for a Staff College qualified officer with experience on fighter and transport aircraft and helicopters and I seemed to fit the bill.

Soon, there was a major reorganization in Air Headquarters with a crucial structural change in the Maintenance Branch. Three posts of Assistant Chiefs of Air Staff of the rank of Air Vice Marshals were established. They would report directly to the AOM. The three posts were designated as ACAS (Engineering), ACAS (Systems) and ACAS (Logistics Management). AVM Maria was appointed as ACAS (Engg.), AVM Narasimhan as ACAS (Systems) and AVM GB Singh as ACAS (LM). A new Directorate, reporting directly to the AOM and named the Directorate of Maintenance Plans was created. Air Commodore JJ (Pop) Bouche was appointed as the DMP. This directorate would function as the think tank of the AOM besides being the coordinator among the three ACAS's. Three bright wing commanders were appointed as Deputy Directors under the DMP. They were Wg Cdr BK Mukherjee of the AE (M) branch, Wg Cdr NK Nair of the AE (L) branch and Wg Cdr Ramakrishnan of the Logistics branch. This rationalized the entire set up of the Maintenance Branch at Air Headquarters.

After a year, in 1971, a delegation named 'Evaluation and Negotiating Team' for the induction of Mi-8 Helicopters was sent to Moscow, headed by Air Cmde Bouche. The other members of the delegation were Wg Cdr DS Mishra, Sqn Ldr Natrayan and myself. We spent ten days in Moscow and did a comprehensive evaluation after visiting the Mi-8 Helicopter factory and having discussions with the Soviet authorities. Subsequently, these helicopters were introduced into the IAF.

I had enrolled for the BCom Course of the University of Delhi correspondence. When the time came to appear for the exam, I applied for seven days leave. The AOM, the approving officer, was quite upset that I had not informed him about it when I took up the course and denied me the leave. This did not bother me very much as it was not of great consequence.

There was a requirement to send a technical officer on deputation to Botswana. The AOM recommended my name for this assignment, but the P Staff did not agree as the Air Force was running short of technical officers. As a result, no one was sent.

The job of Staff Officer (Tech) to the AOM was a great education for me as I used to be the Secretary for the monthly meeting of the AOM with ACAS's and was privy to the deliberations on a variety of matters relating to all sections of the Maintenance Branch. I also used to accompany the AOM on his visits to various units of the IAF, as well as visits to HAL factories located at Bangalore, Nasik and Koraput.

Prior to the outbreak of the 1971 war, the AOM developed an idea to design a bomb, which could be used to disable the use of the runways by temporarily causing damage to the runway surface so that it became unusable until it was repaired. His idea was to make a bomb with sufficient rigidity to withstand aerodynamic loads for a one-off operation but with enough brittleness to shatter on impact even if dropped from a low flying aircraft. This container would be filled with an Araldite type of adhesive liquid, which would be stable inside the container but would solidify quickly when exposed to air. He selected an officer of the Armament Branch, Wg Cdr Kushlani to be in charge of the project and commissioned the National Chemical Laboratory to design a prototype and gave them a timeline for completion. The project was named Project 'Y' Bomb (after the name Yashwant which was the AOM's first name).

After a series of hiccups, a prototype was made which could be installed on a Su-7 aircraft. Sqn Ldr Lamba, a test pilot, was detailed to carry out a test at the Ambala airbase. The AOM took me along to Ambala and the bomb was dropped on a disused part of a taxi track. The bomb shattered as required and the contents were spayed all over the area. We ran to the area and found that the stuff was solidifying rapidly, so much so that one of my shoes got stuck in it and I had to limp back with one shoe off and one shoe on. The chemical had completely solidified in about 5 minutes and when we tried to remove it with pickaxes and shovels, part of the taxi track came off as well and it became unusable. The 'Y' bomb was declared a success after a few more trials.

Meanwhile, I had got my permanent accommodation at 333 Service Officers Enclave at Dhaula Kuan, close to the Defence Services Public School and Defence Services Officers Institute. We got my son admitted to the Defence Services Public School (later renamed Army Public School). On 11 February 1971, our daughter Sarita was born at the Military Hospital in Delhi Cantonment.

The 1971 war broke out on 3 December 1971 and the AOM got me attached to No. 6 Squadron and authorized me to fly as a flight engineer on Liberator aircraft after a proficiency check. I flew a few sorties of MR in the Liberator. On one such sortie captained by Sqn Ldr VBR Mishra, we flew over the Arabian Sea from Bombay to Karachi, searching for an enemy sub, which was supposed to be prowling in the area according to the Navy's intelligence sources. We did a number of search runs using the antiquated ASV radar. Meanwhile, all our navigational aids failed and we had to rely on Astro Navigation to find our way around. Finally, we were able to contact the Bombay control tower. Since we could not see any lights due to the complete black out, we requested the control tower on VHF RT to momentarily switch the runway lights on. One of us on the lookout saw the runway lights far to the South-West of us. So, we figured out where we were and set course to Poona. When we landed we had about 30 minutes of fuel left. We had flown for 13 hours and 20 minutes but could not find the elusive Pak submarine.

I got back to Delhi after the cease-fire was declared on 16 December 1971. I worked with Air Marshal Malse until he was posted out as the Deputy Chief of Air Staff and Air Marshal Maurice Barker was posted as AOM. He had been the AOC-in-C of Eastern Air Command and had brought his own staff officer, Sqn Ldr Natarajan, as his staff officer. As he was a fighter pilot and Natarajan was a navigator, I was asked to continue as his staff officer until he found his feet and could navigate his way through the complexities of aircraft maintenance. He was a fine gentleman and easy to work with.

My brother Sathyan, on his return to USA had settled down in a small town in the State of New York named Binghamton where he started a group practice along with his wife Rugmini and a few American friends. While he was in India, he had been diagnosed with a stone in his gall bladder, which could be resolved with a minor surgical procedure, as per his doctor. As he was in the process of winding up, he had decided to get it done after his return to the USA. Accordingly, it was decided that one of the doctors in his group practice would conduct the surgery. During the surgery, the stone had slipped into a duct and they were unable to remove it. In the process, his pancreas got infected and he got pancreatitis. When the situation got serious, they moved him to a specialist hospital in Boston for further surgery. My brother Bharathan and Rugmini's mother flew down to Boston. The infection had meanwhile spread to his intestines and they had to remove part of it. When the situation became critical, my sister Sarala also flew down to Boston and we went from Delhi to Madras to be with my folks there. Finally, on New Year's Eve, on 31 December 1972, he passed away during operation. He was thirty-five years old. His daughter Shalini was six years.

We returned to Delhi with Sathyan's ashes, which my brother Bharathan had brought back from the USA. They were to be immersed in the Ganges River at Rishikesh. On a weekend, I drove up to Rishikesh and immersed Sathyan's ashes in the Ganges.

I travelled with Air Marshal Barker to many stations and units and continued as his staff officer until March 1973 when he too was posted out as DCAS and Air Marshal GB Singh took over as AOM. I requested Air Marshal Barker to relieve me and he told me he would post me wherever I wanted. I requested a posting to Headquarters Training Command at Bangalore, which he did. The posting was deferred for a while at the request of the new AOM with whom I worked for a month and then went to Bangalore where I looked forward to have a relaxed life.

Chapter 24

Headquarters Training Command Bangalore

The Training Command Headquarters is located in a leafy suburb of Bangalore called Hebbal. The Officers' quarters were small bungalows on avenues named after the colourful trees of Bangalore like Jacaranda Avenue, Casuarina Avenue, Eucalyptus Avenue, etc. As there was a long waiting list for houses, we stayed in the Officers Mess Annexe for a few days and then moved to an empanelled hotel in Bangalore Cantonment. After a while, a permanent house in the SFQ Project was allotted to me.

HQ Training Command is the Command responsible for the flying and ground training of officers and airmen of the IAF. I had been posted to the Senior Maintenance Staff Officer's branch (SMSO), responsible for the maintenance activities of the units under Training Command. The AOC-in-C of the Command was AVM GD Sharma and the Senior Maintenance Staff Officer (SMSO) was Gp Capt MJ Vittal. I was working directly under Wg Cdr NK Nair, the deputy SMSO, and a brilliant officer of the Technical Electrical branch.

The work was fairly simple and since I had lots of free time, I enrolled for evening classes on Statistical Quality Control conducted by the local branch of the Indian Statistical Institute. On the first day, the principal of the institute Mr Srinivasan gave an opening address and asked the class (mostly composed of young working engineers in the manufacturing sector) to define the word 'Quality'. A number of long-winded answers were given which only partly satisfied him. He finally gave the answer himself as 'Quality is fitness for use'.

I found the course extremely useful. One learnt about statistical sampling, the chi-squared test, tests of statistical significance and various other statistical methods. This was unfamiliar territory for me and I gobbled it all up.

We put our daughter Sarita in a nursery school run by the Air Force. One of our neighbours, Flt Lt Joseph Thomas had a daughter named Rekha who became her constant companion. My son Vasant got admission in Francis Xavier Girls' High School which allowed boys until Grade 3. This was difficult as it was not the usual admission season, but he got in with the intervention of my wife's aunt, Devaky, who was a lecturer in English at the adjoining Jyothi Nivas College. He would commute to school using the school bus of Hindustan Machine Tools, which used to ply by our campus.

I visited all the flying training schools like the Air Force Academy (AFA) and the Fighter Training Wing (FTW) at Hyderabad, the Flying Instructors School (FIS) at Tambaram, the Elementary Flying School (EFS) at Bidar and the Transport Training Wing (TTW) at Yelahanka near Bangalore as part of my job.

A few months later, I was detailed for a five-month course on Management at the newly formed Faculty of Management Studies and Advanced Technology (FOMSAT) at the AFTC premises. The course was called the Senior Technical Officers' Management course (STOM) Course. Ours was the second course to run at this Institute. The FOMSAT was headed by Gp Capt Peter Albuquerque who had done a postgraduate course at the Cranfield Institute of Technology in the UK. As the course was being conducted at Jalahalli in Bangalore, I could continue staying in my house at Training Command and commute every day.

The course syllabus included general management, statistics, operational research, etc. Once a week, there would be a lecture by a guest lecturer and towards the end of the course we had to do a project in one of the industrial establishments located in Bangalore. We visited some of the establishments like HAL, HMT and BEL as part of the course.

The other officers in the course were all senior to me except Sqn Ldr Mohan Raj, who was my course mate. Wg Cdrs Ramu, Sanyal and Kamaraju were among the senior most and Soans, Balasubramaniam and Sil were slightly junior to them.

The instructors, besides the chief instructor Gp Capt Albuquerque, included Wg Cdrs DC Chatterjee and Sreenivasan and Sqn Ldr BG Satyapal who was from my senior course. The course was mostly a participatory one and as a result, we mutually benefitted from the exchange of the wealth of experience in diverse fields which many among us possessed.

One of the guest lecturers was Mr Srinivasan, the head of the Indian Statistical Institute branch at Bangalore and the subject of his lecture was Quality Control. He started off by asking each of us to define 'Quality'. When my turn came up I defined it as 'Fitness for use'. He was a bit surprised, as I had used the exact definition, which he himself had told us during the part-time course I had attended a few months back.

The project work given to us was at Bharat Electronics Ltd, located nearby, and it involved the diagnosis for the high rejection rate of an aluminium component being manufactured by BEL and the creation of a method to reduce the high rejection rate of this component. Our recommendations were accepted and hopefully the rejection rate was reduced.

The course ended with a valedictory function at which the Harjinder trophy for the best student of the course was presented to me. I had an advantage as the course was heavily weighted towards statistics and the others were slightly handicapped by having had no exposure to the subject.

I then returned to my work at Training Command.

We had lots of social activities on the campus. One such party involved an Arabian Nights themed party at which the daughter of a Group Captain of the medical branch presented a scintillating belly dance performance, accompanied by Gp Capt Dere of the TTW. Her name was Miss Renuka Choudhry.

I had to attend another small course on speed-reading conducted by an expert on the subject.

My brother Bharathan meanwhile had been promoted to Service Manager at Ashok Leyland and had moved to a company bungalow on CP Ramaswamy Iyer Road, in the Mylapore area of Madras. Their son, Arjun had been admitted in a school called 'Sishya'.

My elder sister, Sunanda, had moved in along with my mother and Sarala after the retirement of her husband. They had two sons, Radhakrishnan and Sunil. Radhakrishnan had completed his engineering from REC Warangal and Sunil completed electrical engineering from IIT Madras.

On the posting out of Gp Capt Vittal upon his promotion, Gp Capt Rege was posted in as the SMSO.

My course was being considered for promotion to the rank of Wing Commander. There was some trepidation among my course mates as the concept of deep selection had been introduced recently, according to which only one in four officers would be promoted from among those considered by the promotion board. The deep selection would apply for promotions from Squadron Leader to Wing Commander rank and would apply for subsequent promotions as well, but not with the drastic filtration criteria of one in four.

My promotion to the rank of Wing Commander came through shortly and I was posted again to Air Headquarters as Deputy Director of Engineering B2, dealing with American aircraft.

STOM Course, 1973

Chapter 25

Air Headquarters New Delhi

The Deputy Director of Engineering B2 had two sections: B2 (T) dealt with engineering matters and B2 (Q) with logistics matters, that is, spares management.

I was posted as DD ENG B2 (T) and had to deal with the three types of American aircraft on the fleet – the Lockheed Super Constellation, Fairchild Packet and the Dakota. All of these were geriatric aircraft and had myriad problems, except the Superconnies, which had a superb maintenance infrastructure, built up by Air India over the years. The Dakota, being simple to maintain, had no serious engineering problems but had problems with spares and the fleet was surviving by cannibalization. The Packet aircraft had been beset with multiple problems with the engines and propellers. Basically, the engines of the Super Constellation and the Packet were the same – the Wright (Cyclone) Turbo Compound Engine Type R-3350. My first priority was to address the problems plaguing the Packet fleet. I had three technical officers reporting to me – Sqn Ldr Deshpande, Sqn Ldr GJ Williams and Sqn Ldr Dash. All three were my pupils at AFTC and Williams had been a flight engineer with me in No. 6 Squadron. I delegated the Superconnie to Williams and the Dakota to Deshpande and devoted my attention to the Packet aircraft. There was a very senior Wing Commander who shared the office with me from the Logistics Branch who was more interested in organizing his post-retirement job opportunities than in the procurement of spares. He had mastered the art of breaking wind un-aromatically. That was all he did during working hours. But he had an excellent team of subordinate officers, Sqn Ldr Jugal Adlakha, Sqn. Ldr Rajinder Singh and Sqn. Ldr Dhyani, who had the arduous job of spares management for these old aircraft.

My director, Air Commodore DR Kochar, was a competent and energetic old timer, but with a very short fuse. He was a direct, simple man and a very effective executive. After I had studied the problem of engine failures of the Packet aircraft, we had a long meeting wherein we discussed the issue in detail and decided to form a committee to examine the maintenance and overhaul procedures in its operating bases as well as the overhaul agency of the engines. I was made the member secretary of the committee and he was the chairman. The 'Kochar committee', as it came to be called, visited all the Packet operating squadrons at Agra and the detachments operating them. Later, we spent a few days at the agency tasked with overhauling the engines. The recommendations we made were implemented and gradually the failure rates started coming down.

There had been a number of incidents of over-speeding propellers of the Packet aircraft due to malfunctioning of the C2 regulators, which are supposed to regulate the RPM of the propellers, but so far this problem had not resulted in a serious mishap. However, this situation did not last long. One day, a Packet aircraft on detachment at Pathankot had what is known as a runaway propeller and the aircraft apparently became uncontrollable and crashed, killing all on board. I was asked to rush to the spot while the Court of Enquiry was in session and was witness to the gory sight of body parts scattered all over a large area. The court came to the conclusion that the crash had occurred due to the shearing off of the propeller shaft of the starboard engine, caused by a runaway propeller.

The Packet fleet of the IAF were fitted with Aero Products Propellers with four steel blades and were regulated with C2 regulators which had speed governors incorporated in them. These props were the reversible types, which were used while landing, whereby the blade angles could be made negative to provide reverse thrust and thus provide additional braking effect for the aircraft. The C2 Regulators, which regulated the propeller pitch control mechanism, had been beset with problems.

I had some experience on the Hamilton Standard type of propellers fitted on the Liberator aircraft, both in maintaining them and operating them as a flight engineer, and had not experienced any serious problems with them. Similarly, the Dakota aircraft on which I had worked were also fitted with Hamilton Standard props and had no major problems. The clinching evidence of the reliability of the Hamilton Standard props was the experience we had on the Super Constellation aircraft, which were of the reversible type and had the same engine as the Packet and had experienced no such problems. During a meeting with the Chief Engineer of Air India, Mr Jacob, he confirmed that Air India never had any problems with Hamilton Standard propellers during their many years of operations.

A Joint IAF/HAL Study Team was constituted with my Director as Chairman. I was made the member secretary. We were given the task of investigating the unprecedented increase in the failures of the C2 regulators fitted on the Packet aircraft.

We found a number of discrepancies in the procedures being followed at the propeller shop of the overhaul agency, which was under charge of a supervisor named 'Propeller Mani', reputedly a kingpin on all types of propellers. During our detailed examination of the overhaul procedures, 'Propeller Mani' himself was shocked to find that a technician tasked with the measurement of a critical component was signing it off as having been done, when on questioning did not even know which part of the component was to be measured. We could only do a sampling check at random, but it revealed a shocking state of culpable negligence. There were other problems too, which were revealed during our investigations and convinced the team that the propeller system was unreliable.

The team recommended that the flying of Packet aircraft should be resumed only after the fitment of Hamilton Standard propellers, which had a proven record of reliability both in India and elsewhere.

I was tasked with the job of getting a concrete proposal from the Hamilton Standard Company. After some negotiations, it was agreed that the fleet modification would cost five million US Dollars.

What was left was to convince the Ministry of Defence. The file went up and down numerous times at various levels. As soon as it was finally approved, matters were set in motion on an emergency basis and the modification kits started arriving.

The modification programme was progressively carried out at Agra with the assistance of engineers from Hamilton Standard. My course mate Wg Cdr Ramamurthy was the chief engineer officer of the Agra Air Force base and was of great help in expediting the work. After the first aircraft was modified, I flew along with the crew for the first test flight and we performed the necessary tests like feathering, unfeathering, etc., and its functioning was completely satisfactory.

On landing, the AOM, Air Marshal CS Naik, who had been personally monitoring the programme, was informed about this. The modification of the entire fleet was completed in about two months and the fleet started flying operations again.

My Director had retired by now and a new Director, Air Commodore Kulwant Rai had taken over. He was a refined phlegmatic person.

I was allotted a house in Panchsheel Enclave, a nice area in New Delhi. My daughter, Sarita, had to commute by school bus to the Army Public School in Dhaula Kuan area along with my son. We had an interesting neighbour, Captain Satish Sharma, who was a pilot with Indian Airlines. He was married to a Dutch girl. Rajiv Gandhi, who was his colleague in Indian Airlines used to visit them often with his wife Sonia.

The Packet fleet were carrying out their operations without any major issues and everybody breathed a sigh of relief as it appeared that the propeller problems had been resolved finally.

But we were wrong! Early in June 1977, a Hamilton Standard modified Packet with the jet pack on top had a runaway propeller during take-off at the high altitude airfield Thoise in Jammu & Kashmir. The pilot had abandoned take off and managed to stop the aircraft just in time at the edge of the runway, avoiding what could well have been a catastrophic fatal accident. Air Marshal Naik, the AOM, summoned me and told me in no uncertain terms what he felt about it. I took the next available flight to Thoise. We could find nothing wrong with the propeller or its regulator and were quite mystified.

Meanwhile, I had been allotted permanent accommodation at 258 Service Officers Enclave in Dhaula Kuan and arranged for moving on Saturday. On Saturday morning, I got a call from the duty officer that there had been a catastrophic Packet aircraft accident at Srinagar airport on take-off and that I had been appointed as a member of the Court of Enquiry with Wg Cdr Suresh Chand, the Officer Commanding Parachute Training School (PTS) and an experienced Packet pilot, as the President. I would be picked up at Palam airport by a Packet aircraft along with other members of the Court of Enquiry. We took off at 11:00 hours on the same day and rushed to the accident site on landing at Srinagar. A devastating sight confronted us. The wreckage of the aircraft was all over. The sight of the mangled bodies of the crew was overwhelmingly shattering. We could locate the body of Sqn Ldr Clive, the captain, and Sqn Ldr Kaul, the co-pilot, but could not identify the rest of the crew. Some parts of the propeller were found more than a kilometre away, which indicated that this too could have been a case of a runaway propeller. After evaluating all the evidence, the Court concluded that the accident had indeed been due to over-speeding of the starboard propeller.

We recommended grounding of the entire fleet of Packet aircraft till the matter was resolved. As the propellers were still under warranty, we requested Hamilton Standard for help, who immediately sent a specialist from their company to investigate. After a few days, he could not find any defect in the propeller or its regulator after checking the entire fleet.

Air Marshal Naik deputed me to join the specialist in Agra. We repeated all the checks and procedures but drew a complete blank. As a last desperate resort, I took an engine technician with me and went to the cockpit of one of the aircraft and got an external battery plugged in and started operating the throttle back and forth. When I had done this a few times, suddenly the propeller blades went into reverse. I called the technician into the cockpit and opened the panel near the throttle quadrant and found some revealing clues. Normally, when the pilot wants to reverse the props, he pulls the throttles back and then pulls up the reverse lever. What happens is that the reverse lever has a cam, which operates a micro-switch, which then actuates a relay and results in the blade reversal coming into operation. I checked the propeller manual and found that there should be gap of 0.04" between the cam and the micro-switch (called a safety gap). This would ensure that due to vibration the cam would not operate the micro-switch inadvertently as any vibration induced movement of the cam would be absorbed by the gap provided. In this case, the cam was actually touching the micro-switch and it had got actuated due to vibration. I repeated this a number of times to replicate the malfunction and to confirm this. I found that once in a cycle of five operations, the prop would go into reverse. I called the American specialist who tried the same operation and got the same result. We called the chief engineering officer and the squadron commander and they also got the same result. We checked all the aircraft and found that none of them had the specified gap of 0.04". In three cases, the gap was nil – potential over-speeding candidates for a runaway propeller. We got the safety gap adjusted and the problem was resolved as we could not replicate the blades going into reverse on any aircraft. The Hamilton Standard propeller was vindicated. I called up the AOM and gave him the good news.

On investigating the reason for the missing gap, it transpired that the servicing schedule did not specify checking for the gap during minor inspections and even during major inspections. We got it modified immediately. The gap was reset for every packet aircraft in the fleet and the operations of the Packet fleet were resumed.

Air Marshal Naik, Air Officer Maintenance wrote a citation for the award of the Vishisht Seva Medal (VSM) for me, but it was turned down as the last date for receiving citations for the current year had expired. However, it was subsequently awarded to me in January 1979.

In January 1979, I was issued my posting orders as Deputy Air Attaché at the Embassy of India in Moscow.

Chapter 26

Indian Embassy Moscow – Part 1

My posting orders to Moscow arrived on 27th January 1979, the day after Republic Day. I was being posted to the Embassy of India as Deputy Air Attaché with effect from 1st March 1979. It looked like I was climbing the ladder of success, howsoever small the ladder, without any tailwind to help me along. The post was of diplomatic status equated to that of a First Secretary of the Embassy. I was required to get a working knowledge of the Russian language, which I had not succeeded in doing during my earlier training in the country, as I was linguistically a poor learner. One young officer of the Education Branch was detailed to teach the language to my wife and myself so that we would have a working knowledge to get by in Moscow.

I had to be interviewed by the Director of Intelligence and by an officer of the Research and Analysis Wing (RAW) of the Cabinet Secretariat. Finally, I would have to be interviewed by the Chief of Air Staff.

At a personal level, we had to equip ourselves with proper clothing to cope with the severe winters of the Soviet Union, including ceremonial aiguillettes for the uniform. We were entitled to take a maid with us, whose salary would be paid by the Government. We were also given an extra baggage allowance to carry a trunkful of Indian food grains, dals, spices, etc.

All members of the family were given Diplomatic passports. We managed to get a maid, Gabriella John, who was given an Official passport.

I had almost completed all the administrative chores when I got a call from the Joint Director of Personnel, Gp Capt 'Pondy' Jayakumar, to see him as soon as possible. He told me that the CAS was out of the country and would not be back before my departure and advised me to proceed to Moscow without waiting for the customary interview. During this visit, I learnt from the P Staff grapevine that there were some moves by a senior officer from my branch to scuttle my posting, as he wanted one of his protégés to be considered instead.

We departed on the scheduled departure date and took the flight by Air India Boeing 707. The captain of the aircraft happened to be my old 6 Squadron-mate, 'Bumpy' Srivastava, who in the spirit of camaraderie upgraded all of us, including Gabriella John, to first class from the economy class where we were seated. Gabriella had never even been near an aeroplane before. But she was in her element soon. When the airhostess came around with the customary drinks and asked her whether she wanted white or red wine, she casually said she would have the red.

We reached the Sheremetyevo-1 International airport at Moscow on the cold snowy morning of 23 March 1979. The airline crew had announced the outside temperature as −28°C. When we got out of the aircraft a cold blast of air hit us. We quickly boarded the heated bus, which took us to the heated terminal building. After the immigration and customs formalities were over, Wg Cdr Gursharan Singh, whom I would be replacing, met us. I would be occupying the apartment that he would be vacating, but till the handing over procedures were completed, we would be put up in the Hotel Budapest located on Ulitsa Petrovskaya near Red Square.

The taxi took about 40 minutes to cover the 30 km distance from the airport to the hotel. We drove through the wide snow-bound boulevards towards Moscow city. Great grey apartment blocks burst up from the skyline. On either side of the road, there were huge banners with slogans like, 'The Communist Party is the Glory of the Motherland' and 'The Plans of the Party are the plans of the Homeland' with giant pictures of peasants and workers.

We stayed in the hotel for seven days. Food became a bit problem because of the monotony and surfeit of protein-rich food. It was meat or eggs for all three meals with potatoes on the side, but no vegetables, not even once. When we asked for vegetables what we got was more potatoes. We survived on Russian yoghurt called Kefir, and evening meals from embassy colleagues who would invite us for a meal almost every evening in turns. We moved into the apartment vacated by my predecessor, Gursharan Singh. It was located at No. 13 Kutuzovsky Prospect, one of Moscow's most famous thoroughfares, named after Marshal Kutuzov who had defeated Napoleon in 1812. We were on the seventh floor in apartment 135–136 (modified by combining two one-bedroom flats). All the apartments in the building and many neighbouring buildings were occupied by foreigners. My next-door neighbour was a diplomat from Mongolia.

It turned out that Leonid Brezhnev, President of the Soviet Union, lived just about 1 km away at 26 Kutuzovsky Prospekt in a stately apartment building. Above his house lived Yuri Andropov, head of the KGB and Mikhail Suslov, Chief Ideologue of the Communist Party. Andropov himself would later become President upon Brezhnev's death in 1982. Brezhnev supposedly had a dedicated gun room in his apartment. Every morning, his black ZIL limousine would speed by on the way to his office in the Kremlin, along with several escort vehicles in the middle lane reserved for VVIPs. This was repeated in reverse on his way home every evening.

Our apartment building was guarded by a militia-man (police officer) whose only job seemed to be to prevent ordinary Russians from entering the building. Even my son's teenage friends were not allowed in, but he would turn a blind eye when my daughter brought her nine- and ten-year-old friends home. He was human after all!

The embassy was located on a street named Ulitsa Obukha. It had somewhat of a history – in 1812 Napoleon had spent a night in one of the small buildings located in what is now the ambassador's garden, now called Napoleon's Dacha. There was a squash court right next to it that was frequented by embassy personnel, and Vasant would often play squash there with his friends. The embassy had an Army, a Naval and an Air Force wing in addition to the Consular Wing, the Political Wing and the Economic Wing. The Defence Ministry was represented by the Counsellor (Co-ord).

The Air Attaché was Air Cmde SK Mehra, a fighter pilot who later became the Chief of Air Staff. The Army wing was headed by Brig. Satnam Singh, an artillery officer and the Naval Wing by Cmde. Vasudeva, a submariner. The ambassador, Mr Inder Kumar Gujral, who later became the Prime Minister of India, headed the embassy. I landed up in this star-studded environment and reported to my boss, SK Mehra. There were two other officers from the Logistics Branch of the Air Force who were designated as Assistant Air Attaches.

The Indian Foreign Service officers, as one would expect, dominated the Embassy. There was a Minister (Economic) and Minister (Political) under the Ambassador. The IFS hierarchy was as follows: Under the Ministers were the Counsellors and then came the First Secretaries, the Second Secretaries and the Third Secretaries. The Third Secretaries were freshly minted IFS officers who came in initially as Probationers. The Counsellor was equated with the three service Attachés despite the massive difference in the years of service put in by the service Attachés. The Minister was above the Military Attaches in rank, but they reported directly to the Ambassador. One could feel an undercurrent of friction in this set-up. The IFS officers were very rank conscious. Among the Second Secretaries were a couple of bright youngsters like Ramu Damodharan who used to be a news announcer on All India Radio and is now with the United Nations, and S Jaishankar, currently the Foreign Secretary and the erstwhile Ambassador to the USA.

My work was mainly related to project the problems referred to us from Air Headquarters and to get answers from the Soviet Authorities. The procedure was as follows: based on the subject at issue, one had to decide which Soviet authorities would be dealing with it and then make out a letter, fix up an appointment, drive down to the department, wait for an interpreter/protocol officer and then commence the meeting through a Russian interpreter. One would then have to explain the problem in detail through the interpreter. One might not get an answer in writing unless the problem was serious, in which case the answer would be handed over during the next meeting, which would then have to be translated and conveyed back to Air HQ. The answers were in an ambiguous language, which could at times be distorted further in translation/interpretation.

The General Engineering Department dealt mostly with matters relating to the operation and maintenance of aircraft and equipment of Soviet origin and the General Technical Department dealt with overhaul matters. For matters outside these areas, one would have to deal with Aviazagranpratavska (AZP).

If any matter failed to be resolved at my level, it would be escalated to the Air Attaché's level and would then have to go through the whole rigmarole at the appropriate level on the Soviet side. In rare cases, the Ambassador himself would have to step in, which happened only twice during my entire tenure of three years or so.

The two Assistant Air Attaches of the Logistics branch, who had a supporting staff of three Equipment Assistant NCO's, dealt with matters relating to spares. I had an NCO of the clerical branch to assist me. After a few months, an interpreter was posted to each of the military wings – they were military officers who had done the Russian language course at the School of Foreign Languages at Delhi. Luckily, the officer posted to the Air Wing was an engineering officer from the Air Force of the Electronics Branch, Sqn Ldr GP Singh, who had specialized in guided weapons of which I had no clue. I started taking him along for discussions with the Russians on matters relating to his specialty. We took the matter up with Air HQ to get him diplomatic status, which was granted.

Life in Moscow was comfortable financially as we were given a sumptuous foreign allowance on par with the IFS officers. The basic salary was given in three currencies, a third in Rupees was credited to my bank account in India, another third was in US Dollars, which went to a special account in Moscow, and the last third was given in rubles as per the official exchange rate. The money in the dollar account could only be withdrawn in coupons, which was like hard currency and with which one could buy things from specially designated dollar shops called Beryozkas. This was accessible only to foreigners and privileged Russians but was out of bounds to ordinary Russian folk. The rubles were for our daily necessities, which could be used in regular Russian stores. More specialized items were purchased and shipped from Peter Justesen and Ostermann in Copenhagen, who were purveyors of duty-free goods to diplomats around the world. The major shopping centre was a huge mall called the Gasudarstvenny Universalny Magazin (GUM, which means Main Universal Store) located near the Kremlin next to Red Square. It housed nearly a thousand shops, ranged in three tiers, linked by balustraded bridges and promenades. They were sheltered under a glass and iron roof. We visited this mall on a Sunday and saw an army of diligent Muscovites shopping, mostly women in flowery dresses and war veterans with their medals sewn on to their coats in faded ribbons. One noticed an indefinable drabness, the sameness of everyone.

Shopping was the Russian housewife's weariest chore. On an average day, she would spend about 2 hours in queues. In a single shop, she would have to line up in three queues; once to select what she wanted to buy, in a second one to pay at the kassa (cashier) and at the third one to collect the items. The only readily available items were things that no one wanted. You would find the women trawling the shops with their string bags and men with their ubiquitous briefcases ready to buy the unexpected arrival of an East German mixie, a Polish bra or even Indian tea. Anything un-Soviet was considered precious. I noticed queues where the tail of the queue did not know what the head was gobbling up.

As I did not have a car and had been depending on my boss to commute to the office and back, I got the necessary permission from the embassy to buy a car. As one could not buy Russian made cars like the Zhiguli, Moskvitch or Volga off the shelf, and since nobody wanted them in any case, I had booked a Toyota Corolla from a dealer in Helsinki. Even the type of car had to be approved by the Embassy. The car had to be as per your rank/pay grade. For instance, I would not be allowed to buy a BMW even if could afford it. So I went in for the humble Corolla. I took the Red Arrow (Krasnaya Strela) train along with my son Vasant who was twelve years at the time. In Helsinki, we stayed in a small hotel near the town centre. The big news in the local papers and radio that day was that Skylab, the US Space Station, had crashed back to earth in Australia. For many days prior to that, people had been worried that it might crash into a populated area. We spent the next morning shopping at Stockmann, the big Finnish department store, and then collected the car from the dealer in Helsinki. Tom Ahlgren, the manager there, gave me a quick rundown on the car and I then headed back to Moscow via Leningrad, driving a brand new car for the first time in my life, on the other side of the road! I had so far had only a two-door Herald and a second-hand Fiat 1100. We drove back to Leningrad (now St Petersburg) through the border post. We stayed at a hotel there and found next morning that the car's side mirror had been ripped off by some miscreants during the night.

The drive from Leningrad to Moscow was uneventful.

I had got my son and daughter admitted in the local Russian School named Srednaya Schola No. 591. They knew not a word of Russian but picked it up along the way. Sarita was automatically made a young Pioneer, a youth organization for children that most schoolchildren were part of, and wore the associated red Pioneer neckerchief that was part of the school uniform. Older kids had a weekly military training class where they were taught how to dis-assemble machine guns, operate gas masks and similar tasks, but Vasant being a foreigner was not allowed to attend, much to his chagrin. However, kids from Soviet bloc countries that were in the school were allowed to attend. The high school students had to learn English. Vasant's English was much better than that of the Russian teacher who taught English at school, and he would laugh at the incongruity of being taught English, a language he already knew, in Russian, a language he did not.

We started socializing with the other Air Attaches and with friends from the Embassy. We made the customary protocol call on the Ambassador who graciously spent some time with us.

The Air Attaches had a club called the Air Association, which was composed mostly of the Air Attaches of English speaking countries. We would meet once a month at each member's residence in turn for a luncheon get-together. The wives would have separate coffee morning get-togethers. These monthly affairs were eagerly looked forward to. Once a year, the get-together was a combined one with the ladies and families at a place outside Moscow named Zavidovo on the banks of the frozen Volga River. We would stay there for a couple of days in dachas (country cottages) hired for the occasion. We hired a couple of snowmobiles and drove them on the frozen Volga, and also did some cross-country skiing across the river. Some local Russian folks could be seen fishing in the frozen river. They would find a perfect spot and dig a small hole completely through the ice until they saw the water below it. Then, they would take out an ice chisel to widen the hole and lower the special bait on the fishing line. Once the line was set, they would keep a close eye on it to see whether a fish had been hooked. They would shoo us away if we got too close, presumably since we were driving the fish away with the noisy snowmobiles.

The winter weekend would culminate in a grand sit-down dinner at which the next year's President and Secretary of the Air Association would be announced.

At home in Moscow, 1981

Chapter 27

Indian Embassy Moscow – Part 2

The Chief of Air Staff, Air Chief Marshal Idris Latif was to visit the Soviet Union at the invitation of Chief Marshal of Aviation Pavel Stepanovich Kutakhov, Commander in Chief of the Soviet Air Forces. Kutakhov was twice Hero of the Soviet Union, a four time Order of Lenin awardee and also, interestingly, was awarded the Order of the British Empire (OBE) during Second World War.

The Chief was accommodated in a high security Soviet military complex. He was accorded a ceremonial reception after which he visited a number of Soviet military establishments accompanied by the Air Attaché. The Air Secretary of the Chief, Wg Cdr Krishnaswamy, who was my course mate at the Staff College, had accompanied the chief.

An incident occurred during the visit of the Air Chief. The Air Attaché decided that when the CAS was in Moscow an officer from the Air Wing of the Embassy must be on duty near the CAS at all times during his stay. I had welcomed this, as the chief had been my AOC at Poona in 1968. He was gracious in remembering me when my turn came up to be on duty on the first night of his stay. After a while, he told me to go home as he was quite well looked after by the Soviets and he did not need anyone else, as his secretary was also staying nearby. When I reported this to the Air Attaché, he was visibly upset that I had come away from the duty assigned to me.

Apparently, I had screwed up. I was between the proverbial rock and a hard place! But, then, so was he, as he could not go against the wishes of the Air Chief.

Soon, the Air Attaché was posted back to India on completion of his tenure. Air Cmde Vir Narain was posted to take his place. He was a distinguished officer of the Navigators' branch and had earned fame in the Air Force for having designed a bombsight for the Canberra aircraft. He was an intellectual and was the scion of a distinguished family. His wife Sheila was an attractive lady of great sophistication and was the daughter of an ICS Officer, the late Mr Nanjappa.

One of the distinguished visitors from India was Justice Krishna Iyer, who had come for eye surgery to be done by the celebrated Russian eye surgeon, Dr Svyatoslav Fyodorov. He was accorded VVIP status by the Soviets and was admitted to the Kremlin hospital for the surgery. Mr Krishna Iyer was a strict vegetarian and was having serious problems with the food provided by the hospital. The Ambassador got an SOS from him and there was a frantic search in the Embassy for a South Indian officer who could help with his food. I was asked whether I could help. I agreed and was provided special security clearance to visit the Kremlin hospital twice a week with the food. The other person who provided similar vegetarian nourishment was ESL Narasimhan, the First Secretary (Consular) of the Embassy.

I took a tiffin carrier with rice and sambhar, some vegetables and papads. The judge was delighted and welcomed me. Surprisingly, it appears that he had worked as a lawyer in the Tellicherry High Court and had been a tenant at Kottieth House when my wife's grandfather, Krishnan Vakil was practicing as a lawyer in the same court. He came to my apartment after his discharge from the hospital for a meal and while he was there requested me if he could make an international call from my phone. He made the call to Switzerland to Maharishi Mahesh Yogi, who had attained international fame as a teacher of Transcendental Meditation and was the guru to the Beatles, the Beach Boys and other celebrities.

We had some good friends in the Embassy. Two officers from the Naval Wing, Lt Cdr Suresh Menon and his wife Vimala, and Lt Cdr Nirmal and his wife Prema became very good friends with us. Capt. Muddiah of Mazagaon Docks and Mr Narasimhan were the other good folks we were close to. Narasimhan later became the Chief of the Intelligence Bureau and after retirement was appointed as the Governor of Andhra Pradesh. On almost all weekends some of us would organize picnics in some scenic spots around Moscow. Many weekend evenings were spent playing cards in each other's apartments. A young army officer, Major Devraj Singh, who was doing a long course at the famous Frunze academy and his wife Sheila were also part of our crowd. Devraj Singh was posted later as the Military Attaché at the Embassy in Moscow and retired from the Army as a Lt General.

Once there was an urgent call from Indira Gandhi for the Ambassador, IK Gujral, while he was out for a walk on the streets outside the embassy. His assistant explained the situation to the Soviet guard outside the embassy gates.

The guard made a quick call, presumably to other guards in the area, and within a minute told the assistant where the Ambassador could be found and a car was quickly sent to pick him up. Many foreigners, especially Westerners, were under constant surveillance and many apartments were said to be bugged.

In the summer of 1980, we decided to go on a driving holiday through Europe to London. We had to plan and organize the trip well in advance. The Russian girl, Nina, working in the Air Wing, was of great help in getting our visas for all the countries en route. Since we had diplomatic passports it was not very difficult to obtain the visas. We had to inform the protocol section of the Foreign Ministry's 'Administration for servicing the Diplomatic Corps' known by its Russian initials UPDK (The Americans used to call it Updick).

After the paperwork was done, we rented a camping tent, a small gas cylinder and a stove, bought some canned fish and other food to survive en route as we did not have much hard currency to stay in hotels. The plan was to stay in camping sites and with willing friends and relatives wherever available. Our planned itinerary was Moscow–Minsk–Warsaw, East; Berlin, West; Berlin–Osnabruck–Amsterdam–Brussels–Antwerp–Ostend–(ferry)–Dover–London on the way up and London–Dover–(ferry)–Calais–Paris–Frankfurt–Prague–Warsaw–Moscow.

We managed to get a road map from one of the American attaches and planned our route. I wrote to my friends in Paris and Frankfurt about letting us stay with them for a couple of days. We arranged our stay at London with a relative.

On 29 April 1980, we started early in the morning after collecting some 'Puliyodharai' prepared lovingly by Prema Nirmal to provide some nourishment on our way. My head was swimming with contradictory expectations about our trip with no insurance of any kind, not much money and zero previous experience.

We passed the Borodino monument built to commemorate the Battle of Borodino between the Russians and Napoleon's army in 1812. There was very little traffic on the road between Moscow and Minsk. The roadside villages looked neat and artificial. These villages seemed deserted and there were no cafes or restaurants, only a desolate shop with a sign that read 'Magazin' ('shop' in Russian). On the highway, we noticed indications of upcoming eating places with road signs with a crossed knife and fork. My nine-year-old daughter was on the lookout for these signs and would call out whenever the sign appeared. We refuelled the car on the way using special petrol coupons which we had procured from UPDK at Moscow.

The road from Moscow to Minsk seemed interminable and went straight like an arrow with rare stretches of rising terrain, which relapsed again to straight and level after a while. After driving for about 360 km, we reached the city of Smolensk on the bank of the Dneiper River where we stopped for lunch at a café.

The walled city in the centre of Smolensk was destroyed several times throughout its long history because it was on the invasion routes of both Napoleon and Hitler. Smolensk is noted for electronics, textiles, food processing and diamond cutting.

The rest of the drive to Minsk, for another 350 km, was uneventful and dull, except for some dust-clogged lorries carrying wood and cattle, and occasionally a rare bus. There were no ads, no pylons and no telegraph poles. We were now in Belorussia (now Belarus). Some fifty miles before Minsk, we crossed the Berezina River. We reached Minsk and soon found a campsite named 'Minsk Campsite'. There were some Poles and East Germans who were camping there. We too pitched our tent hired from Moscow and slept through the night. Our next stop would be Brest about 300 km ahead. I realized how big the country was on this interminably dull and endless drive. By noon, we reached Brest-Litovsk, which is the border city between Russia and Poland. The city was recaptured by the Russians in 1944 from the Germans who had occupied it in 1941 during Operation Barbarossa.

There was a long line of cars at the border check post which we could bypass as we had red diplomatic passports. They were checking the other cars slowly and thoroughly, even the bottom of the chassis with torches. We sailed through after a cursory check of our passports and entered Terespol, the border town between Poland and Belorussia on the Polish side. We drove on to Warsaw, which we reached by evening and checked in at a pensione run by a lady named Mrs Lamnik Zolistan.

Although belonging to the communist bloc, Warsaw (Warszawa in Polish) was an interesting city. People were friendly and shops had more interesting things to buy. We spent two days in Warsaw and visited some tourist attractions in the old town. The heart of the Old Town was the grand Market Square, lined with brightly painted Renaissance and Baroque-style buildings. The Polish currency was the Zloty that had two exchange rates – the official rate and the market rate, like the ruble in the Soviet Union. Our cheerful landlady was willing to accept the room charges in dollars at the market rate, so for a few dollars, we could spend two days there all inclusive.

The next leg was from Warsaw to East Berlin, a distance of about 500 km. East Berlin was situated in the heart of the German Democratic Republic (GDR). The Allies had divided the defeated Germany at the Yalta conference into four occupation zones. The capital Berlin was also divided among the allies.

We took about 6 hours on Autostrada 2 via Lodz and Poznan and reached East Berlin. The drive through East Germany and East Berlin was very a depressing affair with gaunt buildings and listless, unhappy looking people. We quickly drove towards Checkpoint Charlie to get into West Berlin. The Berlin Wall was the border barrier surrounding West Berlin, more than 140 km long. The entire city was in the Soviet zone, thus creating an enclave of capitalism surrounded by the communist East. We had to cross into West Berlin through Checkpoint Charlie, which had figured in many movies doing the cold war period.

After crossing into West Berlin, it was like a fairyland with bright neon – lit streets and happy people. We checked into a pensione owned by Mrs Moritz, which we had fixed up earlier from Moscow.

The next day we took a stroll along the 'Unter den Linden' boulevard, linking the Stadtschloss royal palace to Pariser Platz and Brandenburg Gate. We also visited the Berlin wall, Kurfürstendamm and Frederickstrasse. The alliterative headline in the papers that day was 'Tito Tot'. Apparently, Marshal Tito had died the previous day.

After a 2-day stay in West Berlin, we hit the road again and took the autobahn towards Osnabruck via Hanover. We managed to get a spot in a campsite and camped there for the night, took a shower in the camp and rested for the night. The next morning we resumed our journey towards Amsterdam via Apeldoorn.

Amsterdam, the capital of the Netherland is a city of canals, tulips and windmills. The charming city had a number of parks and museums. Rembrandt is the artist most associated with Amsterdam, whose works, and the work of his pupils, are displayed in the Rijksmuseum. Rembrandt's masterpiece De Nachtwacht (The Night Watch) is one of top pieces of art displayed there.

We visited the famous catboat on the Herengraft canal, which is an animal sanctuary that literally floats. It is a refuge for stray and abandoned cats, which, thanks to its unique location on a houseboat in Amsterdam's picturesque canal belt, had become a world-famous tourist attraction, the one and only catboat in the world.

Our next destination was Antwerp via Brussels. On the drive to Brussels we diverted to Zandvoort, a well-known beach resort where we visited a dolphin show. My daughter, Sarita, was thrilled to be picked from the audience to be a passenger in a boat pulled by dolphins.

On the road to Brussels we found a wayside eatery selling fried mussels (moules-frites) with which we were very familiar as it is common in Tellicherry, our hometown. We gorged on these delicious Belgian mussels and proceeded to Brussels where we drove around the city and then drove on to Antwerp and finally reached Ostend in the evening. At Ostend we drove the car to the ferryboat, which would take us to Dover in England.

We reached Dover early the next morning and took the A2 road to London. The change over from driving on the right side of the road to the left was bit of a problem for a while, but I got used to it by the time we reached Catford in London. We had been invited to stay with Dr Karnail Kahlon, who was married to my brother Bharathan's sister-in-law, Dr Jalajem, one of the 'Jem' sisters of Calicut. Her sister Pankajem from Calicut was also visiting her at the time to help out with her one-year-old daughter. We stayed with them for a week. During our stay in London, I took my family to see the sights of London. We visited the Tower of London to see the crown jewels, Buckingham Palace, Oxford Street and Madam Tussaud's. I got the car checked out to prepare for our road trip back to Moscow.

After a week of relaxation, we started for Dover and took the ferry from Dover to Calais, which was a much shorter trip than the ferry from Ostend to Dover. The changeover from driving on the left side of the road to the right was much easier this time. We reached Paris at the peak of traffic and reached the Boulevard Periferique, which is a controlled access dual-carriageway ring road in Paris. I had told my son Vasant, who was my navigator for the entire trip, to look out for Boulevard De Dixmude, the road where the apartment of my host was located. We missed it the first time, and after 30 minutes of going around again found it and got on to it with some dexterous manoeuvring. We located the house where my friend Wg. Cdr Shastry, the deputy air attaché at the Indian embassy, was staying. He welcomed us and gave us a short introduction to what we should see during our short stay in the city.

The next morning we visited the Arc De Triomphe, the 50-meter high memorial to the fallen soldiers of France during the revolution and the Napoleonic wars. We also visited the Louvre, the Champs-Elysees and the Eiffel Tower.

Early in the next morning, we set out for Frankfurt. The distance was less than 500 km and the roads were great. We drove through Rheims and Metz through Luxemburg to Saarbrucken, took a diversion to Dusseldorf and then to Frankfurt via Mainz, Ludwigshafen, Dunstedt and finally reached Bad-Soden in Frankfurt where my friend Madhu was staying.

Madhu was from Calicut and had studied in St Joseph's, my alma mater, and was great raconteur of old stories. He took us around Frankfurt, where he had stayed for many years working for Telefunken, and spoke German like a native. Madhu took us to visit some of his Indian friends living in Frankfurt. We had a great time in Frankfurt, thanks to Madhu and his wife, Gita.

We left Frankfurt for Prague, the capital of Czechoslovakia on the next leg of our trip. Prague had been a political, cultural and economic centre of central Europe with waxing and waning fortunes during its 1,100-year existence. We reached it after driving for 400 km and started looking for a campsite, but after driving for an hour could not find any with a vacancy and finally managed to get a wooden cottage in one camping site to stay for two nights.

Prague was a city in the territory which was under the military and political control of the Soviet Union. The Czechoslovakian Writers' Congress held in the city in 1967 took a strong position against the regime. This spurred the new secretary of the Czech Communist Party, Alexander Dubcek, to proclaim a new deal in his city and country's life, starting the short-lived season of 'socialism with a human face'. It was the Prague Spring, which was aimed at the renovation of institutions in a democratic way. The other Warsaw Pact member countries, except Romania and Albania, reacted with the invasion of Czechoslovakia and the capital on 21 August 1968 by tanks, suppressing any attempt at reform.

It was a delightful city of culture and had a rich history. We started off the next day and visited the historic bridge on the Vltava River connecting the old city to the new. The bridge is decorated with a continuous alley of thirty statues and statuaries, most of them were baroque-style and originally erected around 1,700, enhancing the magical beauty of the city.

The next morning we set off for Warsaw, where we stayed in the same place where we had stayed earlier and did some shopping and got ready for the weary drive back to Moscow. By late morning we reached Brest-Litovsk and crossed over to the Soviet Union. The drive from Brest to Minsk was uneventful. This time we decided to stay in a hotel and relax. It was the end of May and the weather was quite nice.

While driving from Minsk to Moscow, one could not escape seeing the stunning desolation which seemed to permeate the plains of Russia and the inarticulate vastness of the country.

There is a pitiless immensity to the size of the land. The people are just incidental, it appeared. While I was musing along these lines, I was awakened by a squeal from my daughter who had spotted a fork and spoon sign which indicated the possibility of some food ahead.

We reached our apartment on Kutuzovsky Prospect by dusk where Gabriella, our maid, had prepared some nice hot food for us.

Picnic with friends in Moscow, 1982

Chapter 28
Indian Embassy Moscow – Part 3

Moscow is a different city in the summer. From the beginning of June onwards, the temperatures start to rise into the low thirties – which, in a land-locked city this size, can feel pretty hot – and most of the Muscovites spend their time outdoors. We did the same and went out on picnics to the beautiful parks and forests in and around the city. One of the fascinating places was the VDNK, commonly known as Vadankha, located near the TV tower known as the Ostankino Tower. It has a permanent exhibition (Exhibition of Achievements of the National Economy) and borders the Moscow Botanical Garden and Ostankino Park.

There were very few operational churches in Moscow. In fact, it is easier to find a bottle of vodka – the national drink made for the express purpose of getting people sozzled – than an operational church. On weekends, one could see an occasional Russki lying sprawled on the roadside, oblivious to the world. When they ran out of vodka, one could always fall back upon Russian beer, piva, the wholesome patriotic drink of the ordinary Russian.

The Moscow Metro is a glory in gold and the stations are more like palaces. They are clinically clean and superbly efficient. The platforms are chandeliered corridors. Every station is different. For just 5 kopeks, one could go around any number of times. They are so deep that they could use them as nuclear shelters.

The 1980 Summer Olympics, the XXII Olympiad, the first to be held in Eastern Europe were held from 19 July to 3 August 1980. Five countries, including the USA, boycotted the Games consequent to the Soviet invasion of Afghanistan in 1979.

The opening and closing ceremonies were spectacular events. The closing ceremony, which we attended, was an audio-visual extravaganza, which culminated to the tune of the song 'Dasvidanya Moskva' (Goodbye Moscow). The scene was made touchingly poignant with a huge effigy of the Misha Bear, the official mascot of the Games floating in the air in the arena with multi-coloured hydrogen-filled balloons.

India won the field hockey gold medal by winning the finals (4-3) against Spain on 26 July, which we witnessed at Moscow's Dynamo Stadium.

We also saw Nadia Comaneci perform at some gymnastics events where, although not at her 1976 Montreal Olympics peak, she still won two gold and two silver medals.

The Chef de Mission of the Indian Team was Air Vice Marshal Kapoor who had travelled with our UK Courier in 1967 as the Staff Officer to the CAS Milkha Singh had also tagged along as an 'observer'.

My children had by now picked up quite a bit of Russian language. My son, Vasant, while attending the Russian school started preparing for the London University 'O' level examinations. My daughter Sarita had some Russian friends who started coming to our home. She had a problem with the lift in our building. The lifts were so designed that unless the occupant had a minimum weight the switch would not operate. This was to prevent small children from operating the lift unless accompanied by an adult. The floor of the lift was hinged at one side and spring loaded. When the lift did not have the specified load, the floor would not be able to actuate a micro-switch below the floorboard to complete a circuit to make the lift to operate. When my daughter came back from school, she could not operate the lift, as she did not have minimum weight to operate the micro-switch. The problem was solved by a steel rod, which she would carry with her. Their combined weight did the trick.

Vasant's friends outside of the embassy circle were a Hungarian classmate, Geza, a Brazilian classmate, Gilmar, and a Pakistani neighbour, Sadiq. He is in touch with Geza on Facebook. Sarita's friends were her Russian classmates Lena and Veeka (short for Viktoria) and Helena, a Yugoslavian girl. She spoke to her Russian classmates a couple of times by phone a few years ago, and reconnected with Helena as well over the Internet. Helena is now a Borzoi breeder in Slovenia.

Every year on May Day (May 1), I would go to attend the celebrations at Red Square where an elaborate parade was held to celebrate the common worker. On November 7 every year, I would also attend the October Revolution parade in Red Square with Vasant. (It was on November 7 as the Eastern Orthodox calendar that Russia had in 1917 is two weeks behind the Gregorian calendar) The entire Soviet Politburo would stand on top of the Lenin Mausoleum (where Lenin's body is still embalmed) in Red Square to review the parade where Soviet military might was on full display. The military attaches were given prime position just to the right of the mausoleum and we could look up and see Brezhnev being propped up as he was doddering and not able to stand for long durations at this stage. It used to be so cold that our toes invariably froze, since we had to stand without moving in the extreme cold for several hours.

There was not much in the way of entertainment in Moscow. There was very little entertainment on Russian TV, but fortunately the VCR had just become mainstream and we would get videocassettes of movies from others and watch movies at home. David, a Nigerian military attaché, frequently went to London and would lend us tapes of British TV programmes. Also, the Americans would often invite us to watch movies in their homes, projected on the walls using 16-mm sound projectors. There was also not much in the way of eating out. There were cafeteria style places ('stolovayas') and very formal restaurants but nothing much in-between. There was not a single Indian or Chinese restaurant in the entire city!

English books were not to be found in the city. However, the American Embassy periodically had book sales which we would attend without fail. The Air Attaché's office subscribed to Time, Newsweek and popular Indian magazines, which were shared by the officers. Air Cmde Vir Narain also started subscribing to a highbrow literary magazine called Encounter. Vasant later found out that it was covertly funded by the CIA. The BBC World Service was easily audible, contrary to stories that the Soviets were jamming it. I think they jammed only the Russian-language BBC broadcasts.

A year after our last motoring trip to London, I started itching for a second trip to the Southern areas of Europe. After some deliberations, we decided on an itinerary with Rome as the principal destination.

The itinerary finalized was Moscow–Kiev–Lvov–Budapest–Vienna–Venice–Florence–Rome–Pisa–Genoa–Monte Carlo–Nice–Geneva–Interlaken–Frankfurt–Warsaw–Moscow.

We started our 800 km trip to Kiev early on a summer morning in July and drove non-stop for about 4 hours and then stopped at Orel in a camping site. Our next halt was at Kiev. We managed to get a spot in a nice camping site in Kiev. I had visited the city earlier when the Soviet authorities took the military attaches posted to Moscow to visit a military institution located in Kiev.

Kiev was the third largest city in the Soviet Union, 'the mother of Russian cities', as the Russians affectionately called it although it was not really Russian. It is the capital of Ukraine, the granary of the Soviet Union. The city of Kiev was the strategic lodestar for the Germans in 1941. There were war memorials all over the city.

After a stay in Kiev for a day, we set out for Lvov. The distance from Kiev to Lvov was about 450 km over the Carpathian Mountains. The city of Lvov is located in Western Ukraine and had to suffer under the rule of Poland and Russia. The city had a dilapidated charm about it. We drove on through Lvov and reached the border town of Chop and crossed over to Hungary, and after driving non-stop for 250 km reached Budapest.

Budapest is one of the most beautiful cities in the world. We took a walk on the banks of the Danube and visited the Hero's square. The Millennium underground railway of Budapest is the second oldest metro in the world.

We had found a good campsite on the outskirts of the city and pitched our camping tent rented from Moscow. As we were settling down, some Hungarian students who were staying in a nearby tent befriended us and offered to sell us a nice spare tent they had with them, if we paid them in hard currency. We immediately jumped at the deal as the tent we had rented from Moscow was in pathetic condition. We became very friendly with these people who even took Vasant to a local disco.

We visited the main thoroughfares of Ulloi Utca and Vaci Utca and drove across Arpad Bridge to the small island in the middle of the Danube, Margit Sziget, where a cop stopped me for a minor traffic violation. Once he saw the CD sticker on the car, however, he let me go. We stayed only two days in Budapest and hit the road again towards Vienna.

Vienna, the capital of Austria is considered one of the most liveable cities in the world. We got a campsite near the airport and while we were pitching our new Hungarian tent, we saw an Indian couple practicing driving their car in an open area close to the airport.

We drove around a bit and visited the Belvedere palace complex of the Habsburg dynasty. Some of the world's greatest musicians like Schubert and Strauss were born in Austria – and thus was Adolf Hitler!

After Vienna, we drove to Salzburg and setup camp in a campsite. Salzburg's 'Old Town' (Altstadt) is internationally renowned for its baroque architecture and is one of the best-preserved city centres North of the Alps. We visited Mozart's house and walked around the quaint streets. The Sound of Music was filmed in the surrounding hills.

We set out for Venice the next morning. We visited St Mark's square and also saw the glassmakers making blown glassware. The highways in Italy were fast to drive on, but they were expensive because of the toll charges. So we went off the highway and took the smaller roads and reached Florence, where it was impossible to get any campsite. Finally, we managed to get a seedy one and then stepped out to see the local sights. This riverside city is magnetic, romantic and busy with tourists. We visited the Cuomo, saw the Piazza Michelangelo and spent the rest of the time walking around this beautiful city.

Our next halt was Rome, where we stayed with my wife's cousin Prabha, who had married an Italian and had lived there for many years. We stayed with them for a week and went around the city, delighted with the sights of the world's most seductive and thrilling city. The artistic grandeur of the city was overpowering. We visited the Coliseum, the Pantheon, the Trevi fountain, the Forum, the Vatican, the Sistine Chapel, St Peter's Cathedral and ate and drank some great food and wine.

Prabha was the daughter of my wife's maternal uncle, Kottieth Lakshmanan, who was from the Defence Science Organization and was the Scientific Advisor to the Chief of Army Staff. She was an adventurous, footloose type of girl and after her graduation from Wadia College in Poona, she had moved to Delhi with her parents. After a while, she decided to make a trip to Europe. To get over the problems of the elaborate formalities required to go abroad at that time in 1967, she decided to board a merchant ship named SS Saldana as a sleeping-bag passenger along with a couple of boys, one from St Stephens and the other a dropout from IIT Kharagpur.

After six days, they landed at Khorramshahr, a port in Iran. She got in touch with Mr KV Padmanabhan, a distant relative who was the Indian ambassador to Iran, who sent a consular officer to escort her to Tehran. She stayed at the Ambassador's residence for a week and then went to her aunt in Kuwait who was teaching in the Indo-Pakistan school there. She borrowed a hundred dollars from her aunt and boarded a bus to Istanbul. At Istanbul, she got into the Orient Express train and got off at Trieste and finally landed up in Rome, where she contacted Mrs Outza Chatterjee, the Italian wife of Colonel (Dr) Chatterjee, a family friend of her parents. She stayed with her for a few days and then moved into a pensione where one of her Delhi friends was staying. This boy was from the Royal family of Bhind in Madhya Pradesh and was working as the English announcer for Vatican Radio. Soon thereafter, he got a summons from his father in Bhind to come back to India, as he was required to get back for his coronation as the Yuvraj of Bhind. Before leaving, he offered his job to Prabha and she became the English News announcer at the Vatican radio station. After a few years, she got a ground job in Air India. Soon after, she got married to Marco Gili, a handsome Italian boy.

We had a great time with Prabha, Marco and their small children, Matteo and Maya Julia. From Rome, we left for Pisa and after a trip to the Leaning Tower and climbing to the top, drove on to Monte Carlo through Genoa. We drove through Monte Carlo, with its celebrated casino and upmarket hotels, where we did not linger and with parsimonious restraint, drove on to Nice, where we spent the night in a nice but expensive camping site. The next day we drove on to the international tourist resort of Interlaken in the Swiss Alps. We took a delightful ropeway car ride in Interlaken along with a number of tourists.

Vasant's favourite thing to do in Europe was to take pictures standing in front of fancy sports cars. We have several examples of it in our photo albums.

Our next stop was Geneva where we pitched our tent on the banks of Lake Geneva and just relaxed. Geneva is one of the most expensive cities in the world. We just drove around the city admiring the cosy picture post card houses, with flowers all around them. The tidiness and chicness of all towns in Switzerland was pretty impressive. We could not stay for long in this country of luxury watches, chocolates and bank secrecy.

From Geneva we drove to Frankfurt, and stayed at Bad-Soden with Madhu Paroor and after a couple of days of shopping and relaxing at Madhu's place took off for Warsaw and stayed there for a day. Madhu subsequently visited us in Moscow the following summer along with his family as part of a road trip.

We decided to start early for the last leg of our trip and drove straight through without stopping at Minsk like last time, and drove directly to

Moscow. It took us about 12 hours of driving time but we made it because of the 'get homeitis' syndrome. Shortly thereafter I resumed my job in the Embassy.

The intensity of our activities in the Embassy increases manifoldly when delegations arrive. The first delegation was for the AN-32 transport aircraft deal. The delegation was headed by the Joint Secretary of the Ministry of Defence, Mr Desai and had as members, Air Cmde Johnny Greene (Director of Policy and Plans at Air HQ) and Mr Sushil Pillai, the Deputy Secretary in the MOD and some other Air Force Officers. The deal was signed and shortly the Air Force pilots and engineers started arriving for training. Preliminary work for the visit of the delegation and the follow-up after they left had to be done by us in the Air Wing.

Later, Air Cmde P Singh had come for evaluation of the Mig-23 BN aircraft followed by the arrival of Wg Cdr PM Ramachandran and Sqn Ldr Philip Raj Kumar, both well-known test pilots of the Air Force in connection with the evaluation of the Mig-25 and Mig-23 MF. Air Vice Marshal Katre also arrived with a team for finalizing the contract for these aircraft, and to evaluate the Mig-27 and Mig-29 aircraft.

Another delegation headed by Air Cmde Lamba, the test pilot who had tested the Y bomb, the brain-child of Air Marshal Malse, arrived to evaluate the Il-76 Heavy Transport aircraft. I accompanied the delegation to Fergana in Uzbekistan and flew with them in the aircraft. An impressive demonstration of the capability of this aircraft was shown to us, which included the airdropping of large number parachutists followed the dropping of a big Zil truck by parachute.

Part of our job as military diplomats involved entertaining and getting entertained by other diplomats. We had to reciprocate the hospitality of others who invited us for dinner to their homes. A representational grant was given to us to defray the expenses for these activities. Besides the diplomats of other countries, we had to invite the Soviet Air Force Officers with whom we had professional dealings like officers of the GED, GTD and Aviaexport.

The procedure for inviting the Soviets was not simple. One makes out the list of the people invited and hands it over to the protocol department of the organization. We would invite the wives as well, as is the normal custom. On the day specified, they would all arrive at your place in a group with some people whom you had not invited as well, but none would come with their wives. The leader of the group would hand over a bouquet of flowers to the lady of the house. Drinks would be served, usually Scotch whisky, their universal preference. But in every such group, one person would decline any alcoholic beverages, possibly to keep a watch on the others. They loved Indian food, particularly samosas and fried papads, which used to be in great demand as snacks. Once the party warmed up, they would relax and even occasionally break into song. The person who did not drink (probably a KGB guy) would decide to have dinner served and after the postprandial cognac, they would all leave together.

The dinner with Western diplomats would almost always be sit-down affairs and after a pre-dinner drink or two we would sit at the designated places at the dining table. Wine would invariably be served and cognac and champagne would also be an option. The invitation would specify the time as 8:15 pm. and it was de rigueur that guests should arrive on time or not more than 5 minutes early or late.

All the countries celebrated their national days or their military days, for which we would get invitations. They would be lavish affairs with gourmet food and drinks, dinner and dancing. Everybody would look forward for these functions, particularly those hosted by the US and Chinese Embassies.

In 1981, we were sanctioned leave to go home to India. We spent about three weeks in Madras with our folks. My son, Vasant did not come with us, as he had his O level exams.

We had been discussing with the Soviets about the possibility of having an Indian participate in their space programme. A delegation from the Indian Space organization had arrived to finalize the details. I had to accompany this delegation to the Yuri Gagarin Cosmonaut Training Centre (GCTC) at Star City, the training centre for Soviet cosmonauts. The Director of Medical Services of the IAF, DMS (Air), Air Vice Marshal Mulk Raj was part of the delegation. Star City had two sections – the training facility and the residential section for the cosmonauts and their families. Later in September 1982, two test pilots from the IAF, Sqn Ldrs Rakesh Sharma and Ravish Malhotra would undergo two years training as cosmonauts at the Star City. At one of the parties at the Air Attaché's house, Vasant got to meet two cosmonauts: Vladimir Shatalov, Commander of cosmonaut training and Aleksei Yeliseyev and he was very excited.

Prime Minister Morarji Desai had visited Moscow in June 1979 and Vasant was very excited to go to the airport with other embassy families, where both Brezhnev and Prime Minister Kosygin received the Prime Minister. Indira Gandhi visited Moscow in September 1982, after Vasant had returned to India. Sarita was chosen as one of the young girls to give bouquets of flowers to the dignitaries at the airport. She gave hers to Brezhnev and he bent down and kissed her as was the custom. Our relatives in India saw her picture in the Indian Express and kept the cutting for us.

Vasant had appeared for the O level examination of London University from the British Embassy and had passed with straight A's in all subjects except Hindi for which he got a B grade.

On 1 March 1982, I would be completing my three-year tenure in Moscow and as expected, my posting orders came through, posting me as the Chief Engineering Officer of Air Force Station Agra on promotion to the rank of Group Captain. However, this did not materialize as the Embassy requested Air HQ to defer my posting since I was involved in the arrangements being made for the training of our cosmonauts. Air Headquarters, while agreeing to this, confirmed that my seniority as a Group Captain would be protected.

We had to send my son, Vasant, back to India to get him admitted to school before the session started.

Our maid, Gabriella was also keen to get back to India as her contract with us had expired. After she left, we got a Russian girl named Maria through UPDK She was a medical student on a sabbatical and her husband was a taxi driver. She proved to be an excellent cook and even helped my daughter with her homework.

Meanwhile, the Air Attaché was posted out on promotion to Air Vice Marshal and Air Cmde 'Supy' Kaul was posted in as the new Air Attaché.

After a couple of months, my new posting came through as the Commanding officer of Air Force Station Sulur near Coimbatore.

I had to organize a few things before I could move. I had to sell my car or take it to India. It made sense to sell it in Moscow as the car had piled up a lot of mileage and one could get a very good price for it in rubles. The rule was that one could repatriate to India whatever I had spent for buying it in dollars at the official exchange rate. This was very good deal as one could get in rubles much more than the cost price of the car – usually from non-diplomatic staff of other embassies. I spread the word around and one person named Casamir from an African country called Upper Volta (now renamed Burkina Faso) offered a large sum of rubles for the car. So I sold it to him and deposited the repatriable amount to the Embassy to arrange for its repatriation in Indian Rupees. The surplus rubles were busted up in Moscow mostly for buying Russian junk and for paying for our container (Lift Van) for the luggage. The parallel economy was quite widely prevalent in the Soviet Union to enable the generation of so many rubles, particularly for countries like Upper Volta.

My replacement officer, Wg. Cdr Chadha, arrived and after the usual formalities we left for Delhi along with my wife and daughter and a Russian dog named Bruno.

Comrade Bruno, our Russian terrier, 1982

October Revolution Parade, Red Square, 1981

With Soviet cosmonauts in Star City Cosmonaut Training Centre, Moscow, 1981

In Rome with Prabha and family, 1981

Chapter 29

No. 5 BRD Air Force Station Sulur

We bade goodbye to Moscow after a series of farewell parties and boarded the Air India flight to Delhi along with Bruno, our Tibetan terrier that we had bought from a Russian during that winter. We had to get him examined by a vet, got a 'passport' made for him and made a cage in which he would be able to execute 360 degree turn – all this to comply with Soviet animal export regulations. He would not be permitted to accompany us in the cabin as per Air India regulations, but had to be put along with the luggage in the baggage hold.

Luckily, it was not a non-stop flight to Delhi. There was an interim stop at Amritsar. The airline crew permitted us to feed him at Amritsar airport and one dog lover among the cabin-crew had a meal ready for him. But as soon as the cage was opened, Bruno jumped out and ran away into the darkness of the Amritsar airport tarmac. We eventually managed to rescue him and feed him and put him back in the cage and back in the luggage hold.

At Delhi airport, they wanted to keep him in quarantine, but we managed to convince them with the Russian documents we had with us and only then was he released to us.

We stayed in Delhi until the unaccompanied baggage arrived and after getting it cleared, got debriefed at Air HQ. I was asked to report to the AOC-in-C of Maintenance Command, Air Marshal Chaabra, who would be my boss in the line of command. I flew down to Nagpur and reported to him. He was furious with me for the delay in Delhi and would not listen to my legitimate reason for the delay being due to the collection of my unaccompanied baggage. He told me that he had recently sacked another commanding officer of a BRD for not meeting his expectations. He was most probably following the old management precept that by terrorizing your employees you could get the maximum output from them. I was completely disoriented by this approach and knew this was not going to be the beginning of a beautiful relationship. I took the next flight to Coimbatore to take over as the Commanding Officer of No. 5 BRD at Sulur. The equatorial warmth of Coimbatore was a bit unsettling for a few days. This would be my sunset assignment as I was approaching the superannuation age of my substantive rank.

The incumbent commanding officer was Gp Capt SS Ramdas, an outstanding engineer who was a qualified pilot as well. But he was not at the station as he was away on work connected with the La Fontaine Committee looking into the unprecedented increase in aircraft accidents in the Air Force. Wg Cdr Laxman of the logistics branch was officiating in his absence. During the interim period, before I could take over officially, a fatal accident occurred in a hangar where a technician died while servicing an ejection seat of a Kiran aircraft, due the inadvertent ejection of the seat. Not a good start at all for the new CO.

Sulur is located in Kangayampalyam about 18 km from Coimbatore. A former Royal Navy and Indian Naval Base, it was taken over by the IAF in 1955. No. 5 Base Repair started functioning at Sulur from 1959.

When I took over the station, the main task of the Depot was the overhaul of the Kiran jet trainer aircraft. In addition, it was the storage depot for Ajeet and Gnat fighters, Canberra bombers, and Cheetah and Chetak helicopters. There were about 2,000 airmen and SNCO's, 40 Officers and 200 technical personnel on attachment from the Aircraft Division of HAL. The officers were mainly from the engineering branch and production test pilots, and a few from the logistics, accounts, admin branches and two medical officers.

We had a ceremonial handing over ceremony and Gp Capt Ramdas gave me a comprehensive briefing. The current year's task was for the overhaul of twenty-six Kiran aircraft.

This was the first command assignment for me. Besides, this was an assignment of commanding a flying station, which was a bit intimidating initially. I decided to make it a success despite the initial reception from my AOC-in-C.

I went around all sections to get the hang of things and had a number of meetings with the technical personnel in the production hanger. The officer-in-charge of production, Wg Cdr Kandaswamy was a totally motivated officer and the officer-in-charge of planning was Wg Cdr Williams, who was not only my student at AFTC but had been with me as a flight engineer in No. 6 squadron and had taken over from me as Deputy Director in Air Headquarters. The test pilot was Sqn Ldr Velankar, an experienced fighter pilot, and a good person with no hang-ups.

I made a visit to the HAL aircraft factory and met the GM and his deputies and discussed about possible bottlenecks in the production schedule. After the technical aspects were studied, we had a welfare meeting where the issues troubling the men were discussed threadbare. Once I got a handle on things, I requested a meeting with the AOC-in-C who was having reservations about whether we would be able to complete the task for the current year.

At the meeting, I told him that we would be able to complete the task provided I was given a free hand in sanctioning leave for the men and if there was no interference from the staff officers of the command in certain decisions I would be taking. I knew how paranoid he was about task completion and I had leveraged my requests accordingly by factoring in this aspect.

After I got back, I decided to reduce the parades to the bare minimum. Guard duties were reduced for the airmen and increased for the DSC personnel, whose strength was proportionately increased. The section commanders were asked to give leave to all airmen as per their full entitlement.

I knew that parades and guard duties were bugbears for the airmen, having experienced it personally. I also started having my lunch with airmen at random as I was a firm believer that the army, and the air force for that matter, marches on its stomach. I made it known to them that I was one of them just a few years back.

Once these factors were rationalized, I realized that certain logistical factors beyond local control could mess up the production schedule.

The situation was like this. A soon as an aircraft had been flown in from the flying training units, it would be test flown by the test pilots and then evaluated. The engine would be removed and sent to the engine overhaul agency, which was No. 4 BRD in Kanpur. The rotables would be removed and some of them would be dispatched to HAL Lucknow, some to HAL Hyderabad and some to HAL Bangalore, depending on the parent overhaul agency. This had to be carefully coordinated by the Chief of Planning and the Chief of Logistics. These rotables had to come back by the time the aircraft overhaul was complete. This needed seamless coordination and communication with each agency. The arithmetic was simple but the geometry was very complex.

After every component was fitted back and documented, the aircraft would be ground tested and then offered to the test pilot for air testing, who would clear it after he was completely satisfied. Once ready, we would have to signal out the readiness to various agencies. Air HQ would then allot the aircraft to the flying training units depending on their requirements. The pilot from the unit would arrive and air test it and ferry it back to the unit. This procedure would have to be repeated for every aircraft we were tasked to overhaul for the year.

Gp Capt Ramdas from whom I took over had an outstanding reputation and it would be difficult to replicate his performance. The AOC-in-C's concern about the capability of an officer who had been out of circulation for above three years and who had never worked in a BRD was quite legitimate. After I had spent a couple of months interacting with the personnel, I was confident of their dedication and competence and repeatedly confirmed to the C-in-C that the task would be completed. The task was calculated based on the flying task given to the flying training units which in turn would be decided on the number of pilots to be trained, which was a function of operational requirements of the Air Force. It was all inter-connected. I had explained all this to the men in the production hangar, most of them were highly proficient technicians on their last home posting after having had varied experience in all types of aircraft.

I had been allotted a nice bungalow known as 'Sulur House', which was the appointment house for the Station Commander. I got my daughter admitted to the Central School located within the station. She adjusted soon to the completely different environment and syllabus from what she was used to in Russia. My son, Vasant had got admission in the Air Force School at Subroto Park in New Delhi in the 11th Standard based on his 'O' level examination results. We had to put him in the hostel of the school.

The other Air Force Station in Coimbatore was the Air Force Administrative College where ground duty officers of the Logistics, Administrative, Accounts and the Meteorological branches were trained. They would also conduct the Junior Commanders' course, which officers of all branches had to undergo. This College was located on the Race Course road in the city and was commanded by Gp Capt Vania, a decorated officer of the Admin Branch and a celebrated Para jumping instructor. We started interacting often and established a good chemistry. There was also a small naval unit located in the city commanded by Commander Lobo.

As required by protocol, I called on some local dignitaries of the city. One of them was Air Vice Marshal Victor Srihari who used to be my station commander in Poona in 1951. The other was the well-known industrialist and owner of Laxmi Mills, Cavalier GK Devarajulu. He invited me to see his fabulous collection of arms, which included a large number of vintage rifles and pistols.

We had an excellent social life in the station. Besides the officers' mess functions, we started organizing outings with families of officers and men. One of those visits was to the Malmpuzha dam and the park near it, which had the statue of the Yakshi, which was a star attraction. Within the station, the Kalpatharu store established by my predecessor was a convenience for all. We also had a camp cinema hall where Tamil, Hindi and Malayalam films were regularly shown. Sqn Ldr Venugopal who was in charge of this did a splendid job. We started allowing civilians in the area to come to the cinema, which besides increasing revenues, created goodwill with the locals.

We had a severe water shortage in the Coimbatore area including Sulur. The problem was partially solved by getting supplies organized from the Shiruvani Reservoir. My predecessors had been negotiating with the Government for getting the Shiruvani water supply extended to Air Force Station Sulur. Their efforts succeeded and during my time the pipeline was commissioned and the water supply situation was solved for us. But Sulur village continued to have a severe water shortage. But they solved it illegally by breaking our pipeline passing though their village. Despite regular patrolling by our police, the problem persisted. Appeals to the village headmen did not work. Our supplies got depleted. We solved it by getting a tap fitted at one point on the pipeline, which, besides providing regulated water to the village, stopped wastage of water and the supply to us was also not affected.

By 31 March 1983, we succeeded in fulfilling the complete task of twenty-six aircraft. We organized a celebratory rum punch party for everyone. The AOC-in-C and the SMSO of the Command Headquarters sent congratulatory messages to all personnel of the Station. My run of lifetime luck continued.

My son, Vasant had been promoted to the 12th Standard and was determined to get into the Indian Institute of Technology in New Delhi.

He had got enrolled with Brilliant Tutorials as well as Agrawal's for coaching. He was doing very well in the school as well. Sarita had got over her initial problems with her Sanskrit classes, assisted by excellent tuition by the wife of the Asst. Garrison engineer of the station.

Meanwhile, I had to proceed to Nagpur for my VSM medal presentation ceremony by the Chief of Air Staff, which had been delayed three years due to my Moscow posting.

The new task for the year 1983–1984 was forty-six aircraft, a massive increase from the twenty-six of the current year. The AOC-In-C made his annual inspection visit during which he delivered a pep talk to all personnel. I found him quite mellowed out now. My old boss from Moscow, Air Vice Marshal Vir Narain, had been posted in as the Senior Air and Administrative Staff Officer (SAASO) at HQ Maintenance Command.

We used to get lots of guests at Sulur. We had invited my mother-in-law to stay with us and she developed our garden into an eye-catching collection of blossoms and greenery. Vidya, my wife's niece, had also come to stay with us pending the issue of a US visa for her to join her husband in USA. My brother Bharathan and his family also came to stay for a while. Many other relatives and friends called on us at various times. Vasant would come during his school holidays. He had a 10-speed bike that he had brought back from Moscow. He would bike on the aircraft runway after hours to see how fast he could go!

The helicopter test pilot in the unit was Nanku Pande, an outstanding professional who was an asset to the station. I started flying with him in Cheetah helicopters during the periodic test flights of the choppers in storage, and on one occasion we went to the other side of the Nilgiri hills and flew low over the tea estate bungalow of my sister-in-law which scared the hell out of the workers in the tea garden.

The local manager of Indian Airlines approached me one day with a request to use our airfield for scheduled civil air operations for about a year, as the Peelemude airport at Coimbatore would be undergoing extension and repairs. I agreed to this, pending clearance from Command and Air Headquarters, which arrived quickly, subject to normal security considerations. Indian Airlines also wanted a suitable building for the arriving and departing passengers. The only building we could spare was the unit piggery, which we had closed recently as all piggeries in the Air force had to be shut down due to medical reasons. They happily accepted it and within a month transformed it into a nice departure and arrival lounge. Soon Sulur airport became the de facto air terminal for Coimbatore.

The retirement age for a Wing Commander being fifty-two years, and as my substantive rank was still that of Wing Commander, I was due to retire on 31 August 1983. I had informed the C-in-C about my impending retirement. He was quite upset that I would be leaving mid-stream during the production year and I was still an acting Group Captain even after a year of holding the rank. It appears that there was some problem of cadre vacancies not being available. The Director of Personnel at Air HQ, my old boss in Moscow, Polly Mehra, called me one day and told me that my substantive rank was coming through soon and told me to hold my horses about retiring. As promised, it came through within two weeks and so I could carry on for a while longer-in fact for another three years till my 55th year.

While we were busy with the hectic activities involved in meeting the unprecedented task of overhauling forty-six aircraft during 1983–1984, we had a major digression in flying activity. The 'Thunderbolts', the aerobatic team of Hunter aircraft landed up at Sulur airbase, to practice formation aerobatics while on a demonstration tour to the South of the country. The team under the command of Wg Cdr Ben Brar got a call from their ex-squadron commander, Cecil Parker, who was the Chief Instructor at the Staff College at that time, requesting him to do a fly-past above the staff college as part of their exercise. They did so the next day without a hitch. But later in the day, I got a call from the Collector of Nilgiri district, who had found out that aircraft had taken off from Sulur and had violated the rule regarding not flying over Aruvankadu cordite factory near Wellington. I called up Ben and he told me that he had done it under instruction from the CI staff college. I called the CI and he confirmed what Ben had told me and that he would resolve the issue with the Collector. Nothing further was heard about the affair.

Meanwhile, we were getting worried about the completion of our task, as there were bottlenecks in the supply of overhauled engines from Kanpur. We were short of ten aircraft in the beginning of March. However, by some superhuman effort and assistance from HAL, we succeeded in test flying and clearing forty-seven aircraft on 31 March 1984, one more than our target.

It was a stupendous achievement on the part of all the men of the station and officers like Wg Cdr Kandaswamy, Sqn Ldr Kishore of the Production Hanger, Wg. Cdr Velanker, the chief Test Pilot, Wg Cdr Williams, the Chief of Planning and Wg Cdr Gill, the Chief of Logistics. During the Annual Commanders conference held at HQ Maintenance Command in April, No. 5 BRD was awarded the best BRD trophy.

Some of the officers and men were given suitable awards ranging from VSMs to commendations by the CAS for their remarkable achievement.

Vasant had appeared for the IIT Entrance Examination in April 1984 and his result came out on 1 June. He had passed with the 79th "All India Rank", which would ensure that he would get the Computer Science and Engineering group, which he wanted, at the IIT of his choice. He got the 24th "All India Rank" for his 12th Standard CBSE examination. He had also passed the National Talent Scholarship Exam in 1984 and started getting monthly scholarships during his entire stay of four years at IIT Delhi. He also got cash awards from the Air Force and from Brilliant Tutorials and Agrawal's. Agrawal's had a trip to Bombay for the first 100 rank holders, but just before going Vasant got hepatitis. Apparently, on the train from Delhi to Sulur he had drunk some water from a steam engine at a station en route, as there was no other water around.

He went for his counselling interview in Delhi and was offered the Computer Science and Engineering Group at IIT Delhi.

After his interview, he came home for his holidays to Sulur where I got him enrolled for a short typewriting course in a typewriting school we had opened in the airmens' residential complex.

The task for the year 2014–2015 was much less than the previous year. So we were comfortably sailing along.

The AOC-in-C of HQ Training Command, Air Marshal EPR Nair, who used to be the Navigation Leader in No. 6 Squadron during my time in the squadron, was coming on an official annual inspection visit to AFAC. As per normal service custom, I was also invited along with my wife for the ceremonial sit-down lunch at AFAC in honour of the C-in-C.

We were seated at the head table along with the commandant, the AOC-in-C and their wives. During the lunch, there was an emergency message from Sulur saying that a Kiran aircraft on a test flight had crashed and that I was required immediately back at base. I excused myself in the middle of the lunch and drove back to base. It appeared that in the absence of the chief test pilot, the officiating test pilot had taken up a Kiran aircraft for a regular post-production flight and during low flying had an engine flame out. As the relight was unsuccessful, the pilot had to eject and the aircraft had crashed. We sent a helicopter to rescue the pilot, who was uninjured.

This was a black mark for the BRD and for myself as this was the first flying accident at Sulur Air Force base during my command. A Court of Enquiry was ordered. Meanwhile, the Inspector General of the Air Force, Air Vice Marshal Sikand, flew down and gave a private dressing down to the young pilot, after I had briefed him.

The Court of Enquiry recommended a lenient punishment for the pilot for unauthorized low flying, and exonerated the station personnel, as it was a technical failure of the engine.

The day after the assassination of Indira Gandhi in October 1984, there was widespread rioting in North India. Coimbatore did not have serious problems. There was a small community of Sikhs in the automobile sector settled in Coimbatore for years. The city was nevertheless calm. However, one evening I got a call from the guardroom that the local villagers had stopped a truck carrying a load of tires from Punjab to Coimbatore. The villages had observed that the driver of the truck and his companion were Sikhs. After some argument, they were threatening to set the truck on fire. As it happened very close the Air Force Station, the guardroom had witnessed it and informed me about this incident. I instructed the guardroom that if things got out of control, they should go to the spot and put up an act to arrest the drivers and bring them and their truck inside the Air Force Camp. This calmed the situation down and the violent villagers dispersed. We kept the two drivers inside the cells in the guardroom and released them only when things had subsided. As it happened, Field Marshal Manekshaw was residing in our VIP Cottage as he was on his way the Staff College in Wellington to deliver a lecture and was awaiting the staff college transport to pick him up. He called me up and asked me what the hullaballoo was about. He told me that I was skating on thin ice to get involved in these delicate matters, but said that he would have done the same thing and shook my hand.

I called up my C-in-C and informed about the entire episode. He was non-committal about it.

Shortly thereafter, my posting on promotion to Air Commodore rank came through to HQ Western Air Command as Command Engineering Officer.

The AOC-in-C decided to make a farewell visit to Sulur and insisted on taking us out to Coimbatore for dinner. He asked me to choose a typical South Indian restaurant for the occasion. I spoke to the owner of Annapurna Hotel in Coimbatore city and he agreed to make the necessary arrangements. When we went to the restaurant, we found the owner waiting for us. He had got the entire dining hall cleared and there was just one table with chairs for the four of us – the Air Marshal, his wife, my wife and myself. He had organized the food in such a way that every South Indian delicacy in miniature form was served in stainless steel dishes in typical Southern style. We enjoyed the meal and the owner declined to give a bill for the meal, saying that it was an honour to serve us. On our way out, the C-in-C saw a vintage Matchless 5 HP motorcycle parked outside which belonged to the owner. The C-in-C was astounded to see it, as it appeared he had owned a Matchless bike as a Flying Officer in No. 5 squadron way back in 1953.

The unit organized a series of farewell functions for me from each section and a final touching farewell with me sitting in a jeep being drawn by personnel of the unit.

I handed over charge of the station to Air Commodore KC Kapur at a ceremonial parade.

VSM Investiture, HQ Maintenance Command, Nagpur 1983

Handing over command of No. 5 BRD to Air Cmde Kapur, 1985

Kiran aircraft overhaul, Sulur 1984

Chapter 30

HQ Western Air Command New Delhi

HQ Western Air Command is located in Subroto Park, New Delhi. The AOC-in-C was Air Marshal La Fontaine and the Senior Maintenance Staff Officer was AVM SK Verma of the erstwhile Armament Branch. I had some highly competent officers in my department. My immediate deputy was Gp Capt BB Bindra, my course mate, who had also done the staff college course with me. Under him, Wg Cdr Kurup, an outstanding engineer who had done the pilots' course as well, was looking after the British Jaguar and French Mirage fleets in WAC, and Wg Cdr Subramanian, with a Mig-21 background, was looking after the Mig fleet. The transport and helicopter fleets were under Wg Cdr NP Singh and Wg Cdr Nagpal.

The AOC-in-C, a charming and handsome fighter pilot, was a most likeable personality. He interviewed me in his office, the walls of which were plastered with photographs of his illustrious predecessors.

There was a fairly long waiting list for family accommodation and I therefore checked into the officers' mess in Subroto Park, quite close to the office in Western Air Command. My family continued to stay in Sulur, as the new CO, Air Cmde Kapur had not brought his family along and had graciously permitted us to retain the house. I did not have a car yet and I had to borrow a scooter from a colleague to commute to the office.

My son, Vasant, had joined the Indian Institute of Technology at Delhi to study Computer Science and was staying in the Nilgiri hostel on the IIT premises.

I made some visits to some of the fighter squadron units under the Command, like Adampur, Halwara, Ambala and Hindon. The nearest fighter base was Hindon, which was commanded by Air Cmde Eric Allen who had been my neighbour in Training Command Bangalore. I had to visit Hindon quite a few times to familiarize myself with the problems being faced by the Mig-27 aircraft based there.

Meanwhile, the AOC-in-C took over as the Chief of Air Staff, as the incumbent chief, Air Chief Marshal Katre, had died in harness on 30 June 1985. The new AOC-in-C was Air Marshal MM Singh. Air Marshal Sikand, his comrade at arms and close buddy, occupied the newly created post of Chief of Staff.

The AOC-in-C started a system of weekly briefings from all departments, which all officers had to attend. This helped to keep everyone on his or her toes and updated about everything that was happening in other departments as well. All officers had to be up to date and vigilant all the time to avoid being caught off guard. The boss man's credo was 'I want only facts-no bloody opinions'.

The major problem we had to tackle was the gas leak from the engines of the Mig-21 aircraft, resulting in the engines catching fire in flight. The AOM, Air Marshal Sandhanwalia, was personally monitoring the case and he used to have periodic meetings in his office where a rep from WAC was also expected to attend. This problem festered for a very long time and no immediate solution could be found.

My family joined me at Delhi as my daughter had to join the Air Force School for her 10th standard. We continued staying in the mess as no accommodation was available yet. We had as our neighbours in the mess, AVM Danny Satur and Gp Capt Khathu awaiting family accommodation. Danny Satur tried to teach my daughter Sarita to play the guitar. As we had our Russian dog Bruno with us, we had problems in staying in the mess for long. So I applied for a lower-than-entitlement house, which was approved, and I moved into a small house.

Meanwhile, my brother-in-law, Cdr Radhakrishnan, who had joined RAW after leaving the Navy, was getting posted out to Rome and was trying to sell his old car. I bought his old Standard-10 car to tide over my transport problems. The car had its own problems. Once the steering wheel came off as I was parking the car at a friend's place in Vasant Kunj and I had to push it right back in and drive back home. The problem was solved when I got an out of turn allotment of a Maruti 800 car the following year.

We moved to our new house and started normal social life. The SMSO, AVM Verma, had retired and Air Vice Marshal Ramdas, who was my predecessor at Air Force Station Sulur, took over.

An interesting responsibility of Western Air Command was to look after the aircraft of the vintage flight. The Spitfire in the vintage flight was in good condition and we were tasked to get it flightworthy. All systems were made serviceable but we did not have the tyres even to make it taxy. We asked Dunlop and Firestone to design a pair of tyres and finally managed to get one set.

Meanwhile as my retirement was due in August 1986, I started looking out for a resettlement job. There was a vacancy for a Product Support Manager with HAL, to be located in Delhi, for which I applied and was called for an interview along with Air Cmde Bidani, an electrical branch officer. As I did not hear anything for some time, I assumed that I was not selected. Later, AVM Verma who was my boss at WAC was selected for the job. I tried various public sector companies who were regularly advertising but drew a blank everywhere.

Just a month prior to my retirement day, while I was having a meeting with AVM Ramdas in his office, he got a call from Mr Pushpinder Singh Chopra, the well-known aviation expert and historian, asking him if he could suggest the name of an engineering officer recently retired or retiring soon, as the Dornier Company was looking out for a person as their Product Support Manager to be based in Delhi. I heard Ramdas replying to him that there was one such person sitting right in front of him. Pushpinder asked him if he could send the person to his office right away, to which Ramdas answered in the negative and told him that he could send him after working hours and gave him my contact details.

Later in the afternoon I got a call from Miss Mirella, Pushpinder's secretary, to ask whether I could visit their office at 17:00 hours the same day. I visited the office at Sujan Singh Park and met him. He told me that the Sales Manager from the Dornier Company in Munich would be arriving to interview prospective candidates and that I would be given more details by Mirella later.

Mirella happened to be the daughter of Air Marshal Keith Lewis, a decorated fighter pilot of the Air Force.

Meanwhile, my retirement orders had arrived and I completed all the formalities and prepared to leave the service in which I had served for thirty-seven years in various capacities.

The AOC-in-C arranged a formal farewell for me and my wife at the Western Air Command Air Force Mess. It was a memorable formal sit-down dinner with a band in attendance. In his farewell speech, he offered me honorary membership of the Mess, which was a very kind gesture on his part.

I was allowed to retain my house for two months after retirement and during this period I had to find suitable rented accommodation in Delhi. Finally, I managed to get an apartment in the Aditi Apartment complex, which had been built for officers of the RAW. My brother-in-law who was with RAW had an apartment there. An Air Force Officer, Wg. Cdr Sawani, had an apartment there and readily agreed to rent it to me.

Before I moved, I got a call from Mirella asking me to go for an interview with Mr Peter Klonk, the Sales Manager of the Dornier Company, at the Sujan Singh Park office at 07:00 hours the next Monday.

I arrived in time for the interview with Mr Klonk. He was a retired Colonel from the Luftwaffe, the German Air Force, and had flown Star fighters. We had a long chat about my background and experience, particularly about my hands-on capability in aircraft maintenance. I was quite embarrassed during the interview as he kept addressing me as 'Sir' as I outranked him.

I left quite satisfied and before leaving, Mirella informed me that three more interviewees were scheduled at different times for the same day for the same job – one from Indian Airlines, one from the Delhi Flying Club and one retired fighter pilot from the IAF.

After a week, I was informed that I had been selected and would be appointed as the Product Support Manager for India to support all the Dornier operating customers, both civil and military, which included Vayudoot, the National Airport Authority, ONGC, Kingfisher Airlines, the Air Force, the Navy and the Coast Guard. I would also have to visit Dornier aircraft operating customers in Nepal, Bhutan and the Maldives as well. This was a dream job at three times the salary which I was drawing in the Air Force, along with a sumptuous travel budget. The job was a contract for two years and it is extendable unto ten years until I reached sixty-five years of age.

I got the necessary permission from the Ministry of Defence and joined the company.

Chapter 31

Dornier Luftfahrt GmbH New Delhi – Part 1

Dornier Flugzeugwerke was a German aircraft manufacturer founded in Friedrichshafen in 1914 by Claudius Dornier. Over the course of its long lifespan, the company produced many designs for both civil and military markets.

In 1983, HAL bought a production license for the Dornier Do 228 aircraft and started manufacturing the aircraft for the Asian market.

I was asked by the company to proceed to the Dornier facility at Oberpfaffenhofen near Munich for a three-month familiarization visit and to undergo a short course on the Dornier 228 aircraft. After moving to my rented apartment in Aditi Apartments, I took a Lufthansa flight to Frankfurt. The company had authorized business class travel for all my domestic and international flights.

I spent a couple of days with my friend Madhu in Frankfurt before proceeding to Munich. The company had sent a Mercedes with a company driver to pick me up from the airport. There was no speed limit on the autobahn and it felt great travelling at high speed through the German countryside in a Mercedes.

They had arranged my accommodation in an inn located in a charming village named Inning, run by a nice old German lady who started fussing over me and led me to my room where a cheerful fire had been lit in the fireplace.

The next morning the company car arrived right on time and took me to the Oberpfaffenhofen facility of the Company. Oberpfaffenhofen is a village which is part of the municipality of Webbing in the district of Sternberg in Bavaria. It is 20 km from the city centre of Munich.

After the necessary security protocol, I was issued with a company ID card that I had to wear at all times while within the company premises.

I was taken to the office of Mrs Helga Driesen who was in charge of the India Desk in the Sales Department of the company headed by Mr Gerd Shoenbuchner. Col. Peter Klonk who had interviewed me was his deputy. He introduced me to Mr Richard Steiner, the Vice-President of Product Support, to whom I would be reporting.

Mr Steiner informed me about what I would be doing during my three-month stay in Germany. The first week would be spent getting introduced to all persons in the department of Sales and Product Support, and spending some time in the aircraft production hangars. The remarkable thing I noticed in the production lines was the absence of too many people working on the aircraft under production, partly because of the automation of processes, but mainly due to the remarkably high productivity of individual workers.

The second week was spent learning about documentation, which was given comparatively disproportionate importance. The procedures involved in spares management and AOG procedures were also covered during the week. Defect investigation procedures were extensively covered during the next week. During the fourth week, I was given detailed exposure to production procedures.

The person detailed for my familiarization programme was Mr Kantsperger, a nattily dressed Bavarian who was fluent in English. His jackets were always branded ones, the favourite brand being 'Gap'. Frau Koch, the secretary to Mr Steiner, looked after all my personal matters.

The fifth week happened to be Christmas week. I was given the option to go back home or stay in Munich to enjoy a European holiday in Bavaria. I opted to go home to sort out various personal matters and to get to know some of our customers. I returned to Delhi and spent a few days at the Dornier office in Sujan Singh Park where I would be working.

Mr Pushpinder Singh Chopra, the Dornier representative in India was the son of Major General Chopra and was an alumnus of the Doon School and was a classmate of Rajiv Gandhi. His wife was the grand-daughter of Sir Sobha Singh and the niece of Khushwant Singh. Pushpinder, known as 'Pushy' in aviation circles, had started an aviation magazine called Vayu Aerospace. He was an aviation enthusiast and had deep knowledge of aviation history, particularly military aviation history. He had a charming personality and was on close terms with senior Air Force officers.

The contract for license production of the Dornier 228 Light Transport Aircraft in India was facilitated in India by Pushpinder and was signed on 29 November 1983. Since then, HAL, Chakeri (Kanpur) had systematically manufactured several variants of this versatile aircraft for the Indian Coast Guard, IAF, Indian Navy and the erstwhile Vayudoot. Smaller numbers of aircraft were also made to order for the Airport Authority of India and private operators such as UB Air and Jagson Airlines.

After the Christmas break, I returned to Munich and started attending the Do 228 course along with some engineers from Dornier's worldwide customers. My batch had customers from Sweden, Malawi and Martinique. Our instructor happened to be an Indian, Mr Krishnan, who had taken up German citizenship and had a German wife. He was from Palghat in Kerala, a fellow mallu! At the end of the course, there was a written examination. Those who passed were given a certificate.

Krishnan invited me for dinner at his house in Swabbing where I met his wife and over a glass of Munchen beer he told me the background of his landing up in Germany. His father was a retired colonel from the Indian army.

Later, I was sent to Frankfurt to undergo a month's training on the Garrett 331 engine manufactured by Allied Signal Company of the USA which was fitted in the Dornier 228 aircraft. The instructor for this course was a retired sergeant of the Royal Air Force whose training technique was very similar to that of the instructors at No. 2 GTS at Tambaram.

I got back to Delhi around mid-June and started my work in real earnest. Our biggest civilian customer was Vayudoot. The Managing Director of Vayudoot was a young pan-chewing executive named Harsh Vardhan who used to be the executive assistant to Mr Raghu Raj, the MD of Air India (a retired banker who was, according to the aviation grapevine, appointed at the behest of RK Dhavan, the PA to Prime Minister Indira Gandhi). Vayudoot was started in 1981 to supplement the domestic air transport network, with a new network designed to feed the Indian Airlines network in state capitals and other big cities. They had a fleet of ten Dornier 228 aircraft.

My first visit as Product Support Manager was Mr Harsh Vardhan. He was chewing 'pan' sitting in the MD's office. The airline was running due to the momentum provided by the experienced ex-air force pilots and retired engineers from Indian Airlines. This would run out soon. I visited some of the regional centres of Vayudoot like Madras, which was headed by Captain Brian De Magrey, an ex-air force pilot and Hyderabad headed by another retired air force pilot.

Their financial situation was in a mess, and despite the efforts of their spare parts chief, Mr Balsubramani, they were short of money to buy spare parts to keep the fleet flying. The Chief Engineer of Vayudoot was MG Sharma, a retired veteran from Indian Airlines and the Quality Control Manager was Mr Nepal, an ex-Air Force SNCO.

I had to visit the company in Munich every six months to update myself on company matters and to report on the Indian fleet problems. During my first visit, they asked me to organize a seminar in Delhi to discuss the Garrett engine failure problems being experienced by Vayudoot.

This was done on my return during which an engine-by-engine detailed analysis was carried out, and the problems afflicting the Vayudoot fleet were discussed threadbare. Mr Otto Mayer, the Company's resident rep in HAL Kanpur, attended the seminar. Mr Mayer was a distinguished engineer who was involved in designing the moon buggy used by American astronauts on the moon.

Mr Steiner visited India in 1987 and wanted me to accompany him to Bhutan, where Bhutan's national airline, Druk Air, was operating Dornier 228 aircraft for their international operations to Calcutta and Bangkok. We took the Druk Air flight from Calcutta and landed in Paro, Bhutan's only airport. Located at a height of 7,200 feet, Paro has been described as one of the most difficult commercial airports in the world to land and take off from. Mr Sonam Tshering, the chief executive of the airline, met us and took us by road to Thimpu. We were put up in the modest Druk Hotel in the centre of Thimpu, a town with no traffic lights and no television. The men wore traditional costumes that looked like dressing gowns. We saw some of them walking on to an empty field to practice archery, their national sport.

Mr Sonam Tshering, who was a graduate of IIT Delhi, told us that he was in need of pilots with experience on Dornier 228 aircraft, and asked whether I could suggest some ex-Air Force pilots to fly their Dorniers and a suitable engineer from India to be trained on the BAe146 aircraft they were negotiating to buy from England.

Mr Steiner was so fascinated by this silent 'Land of the Thunder Dragon' that we stayed on for an extra day in Bhutan at the Paro hotel, which had a lovely view of the Rinpung Dhong monastery.

We returned to Delhi via Calcutta. Steiner was keen to visit Varanasi during his next visit.

During my next visit to the company, Mr Steiner took me to Friedrichshafen near Lake Constance to see the original Dornier facilities. The lake is situated at the confluence of three countries – Bavarian Germany, Austria and Switzerland. We visited the Zeppelin Museum, which has the world's largest collection of the history and technology of airship aviation on display, including a replica of the Hindenburg. We returned after a delicious meal of fresh rainbow trout just caught from Lake Constance.

I was asked by the company to attend the 38th Paris Air show at Le Bourget airport in Paris during June as a representative of Dornier, and to be at the Dornier stall and chalet. We arrived at Le Bourget on 11 June 1987, and after participating at the show for a week, returned to Munich on 17 June 1987. The highlights of the show were a spectacular flying display by the Anglo French Concorde and by the Soviet An-124, one of the largest aeroplanes in the world.

This was a fabulous experience for me both professionally and personally, as I had interactions with a number of aviation professionals from all over the world.

My son Vasant had graduated with a BTech degree in Computer Science and Engineering from IIT Delhi and had got admission at Virginia Polytechnic and State University at Blacksburg, USA. However, due to some inexplicable reason, the US Embassy in Delhi denied him a visa. So, he decided to join IBM in Tokyo under a programme called AIESEC which is a French acronym for Association Internationale des Etudiants en Sciences Economiques et Commerciales. (English: International Association of Students in Economic and Commercial Sciences). He got a year's valuable experience with IBM in Tokyo and returned and got the US Visa and joined Virginia Tech in the US for his Master's degree in Computer Science.

My daughter Sarita, on completion of her 12th standard from the Air Force School got admitted to the BA (Hons) course in Hansraj College of Delhi University.

Vayudoot kept pestering us to increase their credit limit to a million dollars, as they did not have the cash to pay for their badly needed spares. This was agreed to as a goodwill gesture.

On 23 September 1989, a Vayudoot Dornier 228 (VT-EJF) on a scheduled flight from Poona to Hyderabad crashed into a lake behind the Ujani Dam in Maharashtra, killing all eight passengers and three crew members.

I got the necessary clearances from DGCA, flew down to Poona and after checking into a hotel took a van to go the accident site. The DGCA had convened a Court of Enquiry, the members of which also visited the site and we got back after the bodies had been recovered. However, the black box, which would have provided some clues about the accident, could not be recovered. The Court of Enquiry interrogated some eye witnesses from among the villagers but other than conflicting reports about the weather, they could not provide definite clues about the reason for the accident. Meanwhile, I had communicated details of the accident to Dornier who got an underwater metal detector flown in to Delhi to assist in the recovery of the black box. DGCA sought the help of the Navy for some divers with diving equipment. When this was arranged, I flew down to Poona along with the metal detector and reached the site of the accident. The Navy divers, an officer named Lt Ravi Shankaran and a sailor had also arrived. They dived a number of times with full diving regalia and managed to retrieve the black box, along with personal articles belonging to the passengers among whom a newly married couple was also travelling.

The DGCA folks examined the black box in detail and could make out some conversation from the throat mikes of the pilots as well as the area mikes, which had recorded the ambient noise in the cockpit and the indistinct voices of the crew.

The government finally ordered a high level enquiry under the chairmanship of Air Marshal Gole. Vayudoot had got a lawyer to represent them, named Arun Jaitley, and Dornier got a US trained lawyer named Miss Lira Goswamy to represent the company. Since Miss Goswamy was new to the technicalities involving aeroplanes I was tasked with the pleasant job of familiarizing her about the Dornier 228. Air Marshal Gole held a number of hearings and finally it was concluded based on circumstantial evidence, eye witnesses reports, met reports and the cockpit voice recorder evidence that the accident was caused by the aircraft flying through heavy rain and clouds.

An interesting side story after the enquiry was completed is worth mentioning here. The Naval diver Ravi Shankaran, who gained notoriety years later in the Naval war rooms case, had asked Dornier if he could be allowed to keep the underwater metal detector as, according to him, someone from the Delhi office of the Company had promised that he could keep it if he found the black box. This was patently untrue. I had heard from naval sources that he was planning to leave the Navy and was starting a company to salvage old sunken ships off the Western coast of India, for which this gadget would come in handy.

I had to visit Nepal as they had some Dornier 228 aircraft operation there with an airline called Everest Air. A retired Indian Airlines Engineer, Mr Rao, was the chief engineer of Everest Air. They were initially operating Dornier 228 aircraft for the 'Everest View' mountain flights, which took tourists from Kathmandu into valleys close to the rock face so that they could experience the stunning, majestic beauty of nature. Later, they started scheduled flights from Kathmandu to remote airfields in Nepal. They had hired some pilots and ex-Vayudoot engineers from India.

Dornier had organized an international operators' conference in Novatel close to Berchtesgaden, which I was asked to attend. Delegates from Dornier customers from all over the world attended the conference, including Vayudoot and the Coast Guard from India and operators from Namibia, the Marshall Islands, Martinique, Malawi, Thailand, USA, Nigeria and Sweden.

The delegate from Vayudoot, Mr Sunderarajan (an ex-Air India engineer) and an advisor on contract to Vayudoot gave an impressive, controversial presentation and there were some heated discussions after that. The delegates were taken for the Oktoberfest in Munich for an evening of eating and drinking and general merry making. The Oktoberfest is held every year in an area known as Theresienwiese (meadow of Therese) located in the centre of Munich. Large quantities of beer are consumed during the 16-day festival (seven million litres average). Cheerful women in traditional dresses carry the Munich brewed beer in large tankards, five tankards in each hand, and serve the guests who would be wearing conical-shaped Bavarian hats. Food like bratwurst, potato and beer soup, roasted chicken, pig knuckle and ox meat are typical favourites.

On my return to India, I met Sonam Tshering of Druk Air who reminded me about suggesting a reliable, professionally competent engineer to work for his company in Bhutan. One retired engineer from the Air Force was highly recommended by Air Cmde NC Jain (who was a flight engineer with me in No. 6 Squadron). I knew this officer very well. He was the engineer officer of the Thunderbolt aerobatics squadron and I had seen him in action in Sulur when they were on their demonstration tour. The person was Sqn Ldr Appukuttan who had recently retired from the Air Force. He was interviewed and selected and was sent to British Aerospace for training on the BAe 146 aircraft, which they were acquiring. He later rose to be the chief Engineer of Druk Air and proved to be a great asset to the airline.

There were two belly landing accidents involving our civilian customers. A Dornier 228 aircraft VT-EPV belonging to UB Air was operating a flight from Bangalore to Madras on 11 September 1991 under the command of Capt. Harpoon Rashid with Capt. G Soorma as co-pilot. The pilot forgot to lower the landing gear – he had turned off the warning horn. Luckily, the passengers and crew escaped with only minor injuries.

The second incident occurred at Dum Dum airport during a circuit and landing sortie. After a couple of C&L circuits, the pilot switched on the mute button, which silenced the warning horn and he forgot to lower the undercarriage. The pilot insisted that it was a fault in the undercarriage system. We got an engineer flown in from Dornier who checked out the aircraft and proved that the accident was caused by the pilot forgetting to lower the landing gear.

We had another civilian customer named Jagson Airlines based in Delhi. They operated charter flights with three Dornier aircraft but did not survive for more than a few years.

I also made a visit to Singapore along with Mr Kantsperger in connection with a client.

Meanwhile, my daughter Sarita had obtained her Economics Honours degree from Delhi University and got admission to the Times School of Marketing for a post-graduate course in marketing management. One of her instructors in the school was Wg Cdr SS Kaimal who was my course mate in AFTC in 1958–1959.

We had meanwhile shifted to my own house in the Air Force Naval Housing Board in Sector-25, Noida. My course mate BB Bindra, my earlier bosses, Air Cmde Kocher and AVM Verma, and many of my pupils from

AFTC, like AVM Yadavenra Singh, and colleagues like AVM Adlakha, Gp Capt BS Bakshi, and Gp Capt Kahai and AVM 'Rondy' Raina were staying in the complex.

It was good to be back among old friends and colleagues.

Nepal Air Charter Dornier 228, Nepal 1987

Oktoberfest in the Dornier tent, Munich 1987

Chapter 32

Dornier Luftfahrt GmbH New Delhi – Part 2

One of the Dornier 228 operators in the Asia region was Air Maldives, located in Male. I was asked to make a visit to Male and assess the Dornier 228 operations there.

I flew down to Cochin and from there took an Indian Airlines flight to Male. The Republic of Maldives is an island nation, consisting of a double chain of twenty-six atolls located in the Arabian Sea–Indian Ocean area. The Dorniers were being used to convey tourists from Male to the small airports located on other atolls.

We landed in Male, which occupies an entire atoll. An employee of Air Maldives met me at the airport and we took a boat to the Kurumba village resort where I was to stay. Speedboats were the means of transportation between the islands. The Kurumba village resort had a main building where the visitors check-in at the centre of the island, and all the cottages were on the periphery of the circular island. The tariff excluding food was US$ 200 per day, which in the mid-nineties was considered pretty steep. Almost all the visitors were European tourists, mostly German, who were visiting Male for scuba diving.

Although the Maldives are known for stunning beaches and azure waters that typify the tropical idyll, its life beneath the water's surface is becoming ever more respected by scuba divers in the know. They have some good coral reefs, but it is the abundance of marine life throughout the country that sets it apart from other dive destinations.

Later, I visited the office of Air Maldives, which was located on the main island where most of the government offices and embassies were located. The chief pilot of the airlines was an ex-IAF pilot, Wg Cdr Brian de Magrey, who used to be the Vayudoot regional manager in Madras, and my colleague in No. 101 squadron way back in 1960 at Tezpur. He took me to meet the Indian Ambassador, Mr Murali Menon IFS (ex-Army), who was also my colleague in the Indian Embassy in Moscow. I spent a couple of days in their company and got back to Delhi via Cochin.

After a few days, I had to visit HAL Kanpur to meet the Dornier team there. Mr Otto Mayer, the leader of the Dornier team, was doing a splendid job at HAL Kanpur along with his team from Dornier.

For the return flight, I was to take the Indian Airlines flight from Kanpur to Delhi, but at the airport I was told that the flight had been cancelled and the next flight was after three days. I requested them to put me on the flight to Varanasi and from there to Delhi. But there was a long waiting list on that flight. As I had to get back to Delhi in a hurry, I decided to call Air Marshal Ramdas, the then CMD of the airline to help me. Before I could get connected to him, the IAC Manager succeeded in finding a seat for me on the Varanasi flight. I reached Delhi late at night after taking this roundabout route.

At around 2 am, I started sweating profusely and threw up. I felt pain in the sternum area of my chest. I realized that it was a cardiac problem. My daughter called up my neighbour, Wg Cdr Prasad, who was a cardiologist and had retired after being the staff surgeon to the Chief of Air Staff. He examined me and immediately took me in his car to a hospital in Noida. They admitted me to the ICU. The ECG and blood test confirmed that it was a heart attack.

I stayed in the hospital for two weeks. The company gave me two months leave and graciously paid all the hospital bills although it was not in my contract.

They asked Mr Pushpinder Singh Chopra to hire an assistant for me to ease my workload. While searching for a suitable person, Air Marshal Denzel Keelor recommended Gp Capt Ashok Marwaha, who had been his staff officer while in service. I was of the view that we should take someone with a mechanical engineering background. Marwaha happened to be a signals officer. However, out of respect for Air Marshal Keelor, and keeping the larger picture in view, it was decided to employ him. Marwaha was employed initially on probation basis.

After my medical leave, it was decided to send Marwaha to Munich for the four-week course on the Do 228, which he completed satisfactorily despite the fact that he was basically an electronics man. After his return, I took him to our customers for introduction and familiarization. Meanwhile, the engine manufacturers of the Dornier 228 aircraft, Garrett Corporation, had posted an engineer from the USA as their field service representative in India.

He was an Indian and a fellow Mallu to boot, named Bava Naina, who had become a US citizen after immigrating to the USA many years back.

Vasant was completing his Master's degree from Virginia Tech. I took some leave from Munich and left for the USA to visit him in Blacksburg and stayed with him for a couple of days. I took him and one of his friends to Washington where we stayed with a family friend, Dr Radha, who was working for the FDA. We also visited CK Chandran, my wife's first cousin who was with the World Bank. From Washington, we went to San Francisco and stayed with my nephew Sunil Kumar and his wife Blazie who were living in Sunnyvale, a suburb of San Francisco.

We had been invited for the wedding of Shalini, my younger brother Sathyan's daughter who had completed her Doctorate in Pharmacy from the University of San Diego and was getting married to Braden Lynch, one of her classmates at UCSD. We drove down to Sacramento and attended the wedding in a country club there, followed by an Indian ceremony at her mother Rugmini's house.

Vasant had a job offer from Oracle Corporation. After our return from Sacramento, he joined Oracle Corporation at Redwood Shores, California in the middle of Silicon Valley. He took up an apartment on rent in Sunnyvale.

Meanwhile, Dornier was bringing the Dornier 328 to India for demonstration flights. I flew with it to various places including Bangalore and Cochin, where a potential customer had shown interest. This customer was interested in starting a service from Cochin to the Lakshadweep islands. We flew to Lakshadweep along with Mr José Dominic, the head of this company, but could not land at the Agatti airport on the island as it had suddenly become non-operational.

Mr Gerd Shoenbuchner, the Vice-President (Sales) of Dornier was interested in meeting some senior operations people from the Air Force to give an introductory presentation of the Dornier 328. I requested Air Marshal Pratap Rao, the Vice Chief of Air Staff, who was my course mate at the Defence Services Staff College in 1969, for a meeting. He readily agreed and I took Shoenbuchner to him and we had a good meeting and presentation of the Dornier 328.

We decided to employ a field service engineer with hands-on experience on Dornier 228 aircraft to assist me. The news reached DGCA whose 'airworthiness' man in Hyderabad, Mr Rao, showed interest in joining us. He had done the Dornier course in Munich along with Marwaha and they had become buddies. Marwaha was also keen to get him into our setup. He was an ex-corporal from the Air Force and did not have any hands-on experience on type, so I had to turn him down and decided to recommend a young licensed engineer who had worked with Vayudoot and with Everest Air in Nepal. He was interviewed and selected and was sent to Munich for training and familiarization on the Dornier 328.

We had a new customer for the aircraft in Hyderabad named VIF Airways. Mr Syed Arif, the owner of the company, had signed a contract to buy a Dornier 328 aircraft, which would operate from Hyderabad to locations in the Southern regions of India. He recruited some pilots and technical persons to be trained in Germany. The pilots included AVM Mani and Wg Cdr Brian de Magrey who had left Air Maldives.

After delivery of the aircraft in 1995, they started operations with Mani as the chief pilot and GM, and AVM Shastri as Manager (Engineering). Shastri was from my senior course at AFTC.

Mr Steiner, my boss, had retired and Mr Lothar Zimmer had taken over as Vice-President

(Customer Support). During my next visit to Munich, I met Lothar Zimmer who took me up in a company aircraft, which he piloted himself and took me for a spin. He was a much younger man who had returned after a three-year stint in the USA. I found him to be a very capable, direct, no-nonsense man. We had a number of interactions both at Munich and when he came on visits to India.

Sarita had completed her marketing management course at the Times School of Marketing and had got a job in the marketing department of the Times of India and used to commute between Noida and Daryaganj in her Maruti 800, as I had bought a Daewoo Matiz.

A few years after she started working, there was a marriage proposal for her from a family distantly connected by marriage to my wife. It was a serendipitous kind of thing, and after the customary formalities the date of the wedding was decided. The boy, Ashok, was an MBA from the Asian Institute of Management in Manila and was employed as the general manager of a company in Bangalore.

We conducted the wedding at the Woodlands hotel in Bangalore on 3 January 1996 and held a reception in the Bangalore Club the same evening. Sarita moved to Bangalore where Ashok was working and soon got a job with Tata Elxsi as Executive Corporate Communications.

I had been getting regular two-year extensions to my contract and was approaching 65, the mandatory retirement age for employees of the company. Mr Zimmer told me that they could employ me as a consultant which was possible as per company rules, but I decided to retire.

I made a parting visit to the company to bid goodbye to my colleagues in the company – Gerd Shoenbuchner, Peter Klonk, Helga Driesen, Lothar Zimmer, Richard Steiner, Kantsperger, Reinhardt Othman, Klaus Niemen, Vestner and Slizewski.

A few months after my daughter's marriage, I retired from the company. The Delhi office gave me a fond farewell along with a parting silver salver with the signatures of all the employees of the office engraved on it. My colleagues and the staff of the office were gracious in their farewell, particularly Pushpinder Chopra, who was instrumental in my being part of the Dornier family, which included Mr Rashid Jung the brainy sales consultant, Mr Beyond our office manager, Anand the assistant office manager, Priti Johnson our pretty receptionist, Ashok Marwaha my assistant, Abraham Thomas our field service engineer, Mrs Kumari Raja Mohan our librarian and of course Ganga and Nanak Chand who used to keep us nourished with endless cups of tea.

Dornier 328 demonstration tour

Ashok weds Sarita, 3 January 1996

Chapter 33

Vasant weds Joan Ryan

My old friend Sreedharan from 105 Helicopter Unit in 1963, who had taught me how to fly the Bell G3 helicopter, had retired as an Air Vice Marshal from the Air Force. He had been the Operations Manager of the Aviation Research Centre of the Cabinet Secretariat. He started the Rotary Wing Society of India and a professional magazine known as Rotor India. I decided to help him in this venture and became a member of the editorial board of the magazine. The office was initially located in the study of his residence in Sector-21, Noida, but as it grew moved to a garage with two staff members and later to a regular office in the neighbourhood.

I helped him to edit some articles received for publication and also contributed articles regularly. I became a life member of the Rotary Wing Society. The Chiefs of the Army, Air Force and Navy became the patrons of the Society, which got registered with the government on 18 June 1998 and got affiliated to the Aeronautical Society of India, the Helicopter Association International and the International Federation of Helicopter Associations.

The Society conducted regular seminars on various subjects involving helicopters like Helicopter Emergency Medical Services, Helicopter Tourism and also undertook the training of helicopter professionals across a wide spectrum of helicopter operations. They published books like the Helicopter Users' Guidebook, a coffee table book on Civil Rotary Wing Aviation in India, Gallantry Episodes of Helicopter Pilots in War and Peace and many other helicopter-related subjects.

The Rotor India magazine has become an active forum for highlighting problems being faced by helicopter operators in the country and the Society takes them up with the Ministry of Civil Aviation, the DGCA and Airports Authority of India to get them resolved.

During a casual meeting in the Defence Services Canteen, AVM Sreedharan and I saw a notice from the Air Force Naval Housing Board saying that the last day for registering for a Bangalore Housing Scheme project had been extended by a week. We decided to register our names. The next day, we visited the AFNHB Office at Air Force Station, New Delhi. The deputy director general happened to be Air Cmde Ram Mohan Sreedharan, an ex-helicopter pilot. We filled the forms and registered our names by paying Rs 10,000 as a registration fee. The scheme was for apartments in a 9-acre plot located in a place called Byappanahalli in Bangalore. Neither of us had heard of the place but decided to have a go, as Bangalore was a nice place to stay in our old age.

During one of my visits to Bangalore a few months later, I visited the location of the housing scheme and found it extremely well located. Sreedharan, however, withdrew from the scheme, but I continued and a few years later became the owner of an apartment which became Jal Vayu Towers.

Now, I had retired from Dornier, I started visiting my son Vasant who had rented an apartment in Sunnyvale, California. During one such visit, we asked him about his marriage plans. My wife had been doing some research on the subject and had found a suitable match, a girl who was the daughter of a relative and who had graduated from the Imperial College in London. The proposal did not materialize, as the horoscopes did not match!

During our visit, Vasant told me that he had someone in view who was his colleague at Oracle. The girl was from Ireland and had got transferred from the Oracle office in Dublin to the Oracle headquarters in California where Vasant was working. He told me about this at a pub, the Duke of Edinburgh, where he had taken me for a drink. Her name was Joan Ryan and had graduated in Computer Science from Trinity College in Dublin. I had no objection to this, so long as he was happy.

My wife was initially taken aback when we announced the news to her but later when she met Joan she liked her and agreed.

On our return, we started planning for the wedding. Vasant had bought an apartment in Bangalore at Raheja Residency and Sarita and Ashok had moved there from Ashok's bachelor apartment in Shantinagar. So, we decided to conduct the wedding in Bangalore. The venue of the wedding was at a place called Tamarind Tree on the outskirts of the city.

The date of the wedding was 21 February 1998. The balmy weather of Bangalore in February was ideal for an outdoor setting. My wife and her niece Geeta decked up Joan like a Malayalee bride in an off-white sari and jasmine flowers covering her entire head. The ritual was short as in typical mallu weddings, and later we had the reception in the same place.

My wife's niece Vidya's husband Raghu had booked the wedding suite at Taj West End where the couple stayed for a few days and then they moved to Sarita's place at Raheja Residency at Koramangala.

As no one from Joan's family could come for the wedding, it was decided to have an Irish wedding on 5 June 1998, a few months later. My wife and myself took an SAS flight from Delhi and connected from Heathrow to Shannon in Ireland, the land of sad loves and happy wars. After a 2-hour drive from Shannon, we reached Borrisoleigh in County Tipperary, the village/town near where Joan's folks lived. Borrisoleigh had a population of about 900 people and naturally everyone knew everyone else. We got accommodation in a local hotel in Thurles, the nearest big town. The hotel staff knew that we had come for the wedding. Vasant and Joan had already arrived and they came and took us to Joan's mother's cottage. The picture postcard cottage was in the midst of rolling grassland where a large number of cows were peacefully grazing. The cows belonged to Joan's eldest brother James (Jimmy) Ryan. This was an out of the world experience for us.

Ireland's temperate climate and grass growing ability, combined with a dairying tradition, were the natural advantages that made Ireland one of the largest milk producers in the world. Dairy cows in Ireland are generally milked twice per day, with milk collected from farms by milk processing companies called creameries.

According to local custom, the family property goes to eldest son in the family and as a result the farmland does not get divided. We saw the cows being milked mechanically – six cows at a time. The milk gets stored in huge stainless steel refrigerated containers. Every day, a van from the creamery would come and collect the milk after checking the specific gravity of the milk. The milk is so thick that they had to dilute it to lower the specific gravity to acceptable levels. One man is able to milk a hundred cows twice a day!

The wedding was conducted in the local Catholic Church and they even had a rehearsal the previous day. The bridegroom's best man was Vish Ramachandran, who was Vasant's flat mate at Sunnyvale and who was in Virginia Tech with him for their Master's degree in Computer Science.

After the wedding, there was a reception in the hotel where we were staying. It was a sit-down dinner followed by dancing which carried on till the small hours of the next morning. There was a lot of speechmaking during the dinner during which John Ryan, Joan's brother, read out the congratulatory messages. It was a happy ceremony and we thoroughly enjoyed it.

After the wedding ceremonies got over, Joan took us sightseeing for a few days. We visited the cliffs of Moher and the Burren National Park. This lovely land of green meadows, craggy cliffs and the world's best pubs gets into you when you drive through the narrow roads of the Republic which has produced some of the greatest poets, novelists and dramatists of the English language – George Bernard Shaw, Jonathan Swift, Oscar Wilde, James Joyce and WB Yeats.

After a week's stay in this green and pleasant land, we returned to Delhi via London.

Vasant and Joan's Wedding, Bangalore, February 1998

Chapter 34

Retirement Bangalore

Vasant and Joan had taken up a rented house in Mountain View where they stayed for six months and then moved to Los Altos where they had bought a ranch style house. Los Altos strives to maintain a semi-rural atmosphere. It has few sidewalks except in commercial zones and along arterial roads. The minimum lot size for most residential housing is one-quarter of an acre. Most roads have broad dirt shoulders and little or no street lighting. The civic centre sits in the middle of an orchard, a remnant of those that once covered the area. The town is located in Silicon Valley between Palo Alto and Mountain View and is an hour's drive South of San Francisco.

We had gone to visit them in 2001 in July for two months and were scheduled to return the second week of September. On 11 September morning, Vasant came running to our bedroom and told us to go and watch CNN on TV. They were showing the terrorist strike on the World Trade Centre in New York City. It was earth-shattering news. Nineteen militants associated with the Islamic extremist group al-Qaeda had hijacked four airliners and carried out suicide attacks against targets in the USA. Two of the planes were flown into the towers of the World Trade Centre in New York City, a third plane hit the Pentagon just outside Washington, DC, and the fourth plane crashed in a field in Pennsylvania. The attacks resulted in extensive death and destruction, triggering major US initiatives to combat terrorism and defining the presidency of George W Bush. Over 3,000 people were killed during the attacks in New York City and Washington, DC, including more than 400 police and firefighters. CNN was showing the event throughout the day and we were mesmerized watching it on TV.

As there was total disruption in aircraft operations, our flights back to India were cancelled and we had to postpone our return till normalcy was restored.

I had been staying in Sector-25 in Noida in a ground floor apartment which I had bought from the Air Force Naval Housing Board. As I had retired from active work and as we did not have any special interest in continuing to stay in the National Capital Region, we started thinking of relocating to Bangalore. As my daughter Sarita had settled in Bangalore, it was an added attraction. We discussed this option with her and she quickly started looking around for a suitable apartment complex. They had shifted to an apartment they had bought in a complex called Embassy Tranquil (close to Raheja Residency) in the Koramangala area.

Meanwhile, I started looking around for a prospective buyer for my flat in Noida. As luck would have it, Wg Cdr 'Granny' Dhiman, who had retired from HAL Nasik as their chief test pilot, was looking for a ground floor flat as his wife was severely arthritic and was having problems in his first floor flat, which was also in Sector-25 in Noida. We met and agreed on the terms of sale. Meanwhile, Sarita had found a place for me close to her apartment in Koramangala in Bangalore, which was being built by HM Constructions. I told her to book a ground floor flat immediately and paid the booking amount. Within a month, we finalized the sale of our Noida flat to Dhiman.

We moved to Bangalore on 2 July 2003 and stayed with Sarita for a while. As the apartment would take some more time to complete, we decided to go to Vasant's place in Los Altos for a couple of months. We left for San Francisco by Singapore Airlines on 18 August 2003. At Singapore, as the flight to SFO had been overbooked, they gave us an option to go the next day. In compensation, they gave us 500 Singapore dollars each plus free hotel accommodation in the River View hotel and got us upgraded to business class. They gave each of us a gift and a free call to SFO. It was a great deal.

We stayed with Vasant till 1 October 2003. We had a lovely time as Joan and Vasant had a beautiful baby girl, Riana a year earlier, and she had grown into a year old bouncing baby, our first grandchild.

We returned to Bangalore via Singapore. On the flight from Singapore to Bangalore, I had got a middle seat. The gentleman on the aisle seat was apparently very thirsty. After six whiskies and three packets of peanuts, he started generating noises which originated from deep within his innards. This was embarrassing for others and to add to this, he threw up all over me. He apologized and told me that part of the secret of his life was to eat and drink what he liked and let the food and drinks fight it out inside! He smiled at me and I smiled at him, in mutual recognition of bullshit.

We started regular weekend visits to RSI, the fauji club on MG Road, and started meeting many old friends, hobnobbed with angry, grumpy whisky-drinking veterans pontificating with recycled anecdotes.

I met a very old friend and course mate at RSI, a brilliant engineer who was close to the edge of alcohol dependency. He would give me homilies about the mood-elevating and anti-depressant qualities of vodka. I noticed that he had severe tremors in his hands. A week later, he died in his sleep.

The HM flat was almost ready and we got the formalities completed and moved in on 4 December 2003. After moving in, we got the woodwork and interiors completed and decided to have a house warming party. We split it into two sessions, one for relatives and another for friends. On 8 February 2004, after the second party, which involved drinking vast quantities of Bloody Mary, I found myself breathless and threw up a couple of times. As I had earlier history of cardiac problems, we called up Dr Anu, my niece-in-law who quickly came home. By the time she arrived, I had flaked out. She gave me an injection to revive me and quickly moved me to a nearby nursing clinic, which was functioning on a Sunday. They stabilized my condition and suggested that I should be moved to a regular hospital. Dr Anu took me immediately to Wockhardt Hospital on Cunningham Road. It was confirmed that I had a myocardial infarction and after an angiogram they confirmed that there were three blockages and recommended that I should have triple by-pass heart surgery.

I had just become a member of the ECHS medical insurance programme and so the entire expenses of the surgery would be covered by ECHS. My course mate, Air Marshal Ramamurthy, was of great help during this period. He organized five young trainees from AFTC to donate the blood required by the hospital and was of immense help in getting the procedures organized for the ECHS. The cardiologist of the hospital was Dr Ranganath Naik and the cardiac surgeon was Dr Jawali. The surgery was conducted on 16 February 2004 by the beating-heart process and there was not much blood loss. I stayed in the hospital for a week after the surgery and was discharged on 24 February 2004. The experience in the hospital was superb and the after-care was the best one could get. Vasant had also flown down for the operation. The fact that my daughter and son-in-law were with us was a great morale booster for me.

As advised by the doctor, I shifted my activities into lower gear and modified my lifestyle considerably.

We continued to visit Vasant and family every year during summer.

In December 2004, we had a second grandchild when Joan had another baby girl named Nisha. During our visits, we would go to Sacramento to visit my sister-in-law Rugmini, her second husband Dhiraj and her daughter Shalini who had become the mother of two children, Julie and Megan. My nephew Sunil was also not far from Los Altos and we would often have family get-togethers.

Life in Bangalore was blissful. I became a regular visitor to the RSI club.

We started visiting Tellicherry for family get-togethers at Kottieth house. Summers were spent in Los Altos and winters in Tellicherry. The highlight of the Tellicherry visits was the 'Theyyam' ceremony, which takes place late in the night and was fascinating to watch.

Meanwhile, the AFNHB flat in Byappanahalli was ready and I was allotted a flat in Jal Vayu Towers. The flat got registered on 25 April 2008.

I looked out for a tenant and finally got a bachelor who would be staying there with his mother till he got married. He left after a year as he got transferred to Cochin.

Later, the son of an air force officer approached me and I was happy to rent the apartment to him. He was an MBA and was working for a software company in Bangalore.

Sarita's daughter Aliya was born in 2011 in Bombay. This was great news for the entire family as all of us had been waiting for this for so many years. Aliya was a cute, healthy baby and we all welcomed their arrival in Bangalore from Bombay.

On 17 August 2011, on my 80th birthday, Vasant and family came to India. He and Sarita organized a party at the Grand Mercure hotel in Koramangala to celebrate my entry to the octogenarian club. Many of our relatives and Air Force friends attended the party. Aliya was the star attraction at the party. Riana and Nisha also being present, this was a grand ceremony for us as all three grandchildren were together. A rare occasion for me.

My course mate Ramamurthy was having problems with both his kidneys for some time and finally the doctors had to resort to dialysis twice a week for him. Although this was a traumatic event, but he bore it manfully and went through the dialysis every Thursday and Monday.

A couple of years after this, he developed cardiac problems and despite best efforts he passed away while on his way to hospital in an ambulance. The Air Force arranged an impressive funeral for Ramu at which his only child Arjun did the obsequies.

Another close friend and course mate, Air Marshal Uthaya had also passed away while I was in the USA. These two course mates were the only ones from among the twenty-four of us who attained three-star rank. Uthaya had retired as the AOM and Ramu had retired as the AOC-in-C of Maintenance Command.

My son Vasant had shifted to a rented house in Los Altos in 2013 as they had decided to have their house demolished and build a new house in the same place. We made a visit to Los Altos and stayed in the rented house for a couple of months and we would often go and visit the house under construction. The house took much more time than originally scheduled and finally took two years to complete. It was worth to wait; however, as when it was completed it was a lovely five-bedroom villa with a basement. We were eagerly awaiting the completion of the house and had to skip our annual visit in 2014 and did it only on 15 March 2015.

Vasant had started a consulting company called OpsDynamics and he was the co-founder and Chief Executive Officer of the company. His partner was his friend Ramana, a Stanford graduate and was working as a consultant at Google in Mountain View, California. Vasant also took up a job with a subsidiary of Hitachi Corporation. Joan was continuing at Oracle as Senior Director and both their girls, Riana and Nisha were in Almond Elementary School.

Riana later joined a middle school in Los Altos named Egan. They were also actively engaged in learning dance at a dance school called 'Dance Attack' and would take part in many shows in California in the Bay Area as well as at outstation locations. We enjoyed visiting these shows during our visits to Los Altos.

In 2013, Ashok and Sarita moved to Delhi after Ashok left his previous company named ISGN where he was the President and Chief Operating officer. He joined a bigger company, HCL Technologies at Noida in the national capital region as senior VP and global head of operations. This job involved frequent travels to USA, England, Ireland, Philippines and other places.

They rented a house in Maharani Bagh in New Delhi. Aliya was admitted in a preschool in Delhi named The Study, where she became a very popular girl.

I was getting on in years and started getting a problem with my right eye. The eye doctor at Nethradhama hospital in Bangalore diagnosed it as age-related macular degeneration and prescribed Lucentis injections in the right eye. After three injections, my eyesight showed remarkable improvement but after the fourth injection the eye developed scar tissue. And my sight became worse. The doctor did not recommend any more injections and I had to live with good eyesight in my left eye. Dr Mohan Raj who was treating me told me to look after my good eye. I started taking a pill called Ocuvite regularly, which a friend, Dr Radha, had got for me from Washington.

We visited Vasant and his family in their new house and stayed with them for three months from 15 March 15 to 15 June 15. Our 50th wedding anniversary was coming up on 27 June 2015 and we decided to celebrate the occasion with a party at RSI. Vasant came on a week's trip to Bangalore for the party and Sarita and family also came from Delhi for the function.

My nephew, Cdr Vinod Sreenivasan, who had joined the merchant navy after retiring from the Indian Navy organized the party at the Bayonet Hall in the RSI and we invited about seventy odd guests, mostly relatives from both sides of the family and friends from the Air Force and some neighbours from my apartment complex. My nephew Arjun, his wife Aparna and daughter Anahita had also flown in from Chennai for the happy occasion.

Sarita had ordered a lovely cake, which was cut by Aliya who had a great time at the party.

I had started doing some voluntary work in a library located in the Koramangala 3rd Block Park so meticulously looked after by Lata Heble, wife of Air Vice Marshal Suresh Heble, who lives just across the road near the park. Besides the opportunity to go through some really good books donated by the residents of the locality, it was great meeting some interesting people who came to borrow books from the library.

I started hanging out with some interesting octogenarians in the Park. My voluntary work in the library was on Monday mornings and it was here that I started meeting folks from a wide spectrum of professions. One was a liver transplant surgeon, another was a retired Engineer from the Railway Board who introduced me to a gentleman who had a doctorate in Material Science from McGill University in Canada. There was another young man from Bihar who was teaching MBA students, whose grandfather had immigrated to Mauritius. Prakash, a regular visitor was a call driver from Ezi Drive who wanted to borrow English books for his daughter studying in the neighbourhood St Francis School.

A lanky six footer was another interesting visitor to the library. Though he was ninety years old, he could do a brisk six rounds in the park and had a razor sharp brain as well and had a remarkably positive outlook on life. The secret of his splendid constitution was in his own advisory words:

'As you go through life, brother

Whatever be your goal

Keep your eyes on the doughnut

And not upon the hole'

I started writing these memoirs during the three months we stayed at my son's place in Los Altos, when I had nothing to do, as both Joan and Vasant would be away at work and my grand-daughters Riana and Nisha were also busy with their school and extra-curricular activities. I tried re-assembling old memories as best as I could. Once I got going I could not stop and now, six months later, managed to complete it. I realized later that the half remembered anecdotes one tries to convey might evoke interest, which may be inversely proportional to one's own enthusiasm in writing about it.

In this account of my days in uniform, I have tried to rescue from insignificance, some of the small events that made up my life in the Air Force. I hope such a recounting will evoke in the reader a personal response that will cause a nod in the head in recognition or a sudden laugh at the familiarity of what is being described.

My family, 2011

Aliya, 2013

Vasant and kids with us, Los Altos 2015

Vasant's house in Los Altos, May 2015